"We have known Harry and Kate for many years. They are the Having rescued their marriage from the brink, they write with great hone and give sound, practical advice, backed up by the latest research, that will give hope to many couples who can't see a way forward. Everyone will enjoy and benefit from this book, but for some it will be life-changing."

– Nicky and Sila Lee, authors of *The Marriage Course*

"Since we can't all have Harry and Kate as our own private love guidance gurus, we will have to make do with this super book, which is really practical and immensely readable – reading it is like breathing fresh air."

– Richard and Maria Kane, founders of Marriage Week International

"Once picked up, this fantastic book just won't let you put it down! Harry and Kate have successfully combined real life experiences – including, very honestly, their own – with hard earned wisdom and plenty of practical tips, to help us strengthen the most special relationships in our lives – whatever age or stage we're at."

– Fiona Bruce MP

"This book has so much for couples to grab hold of to give them hope for the future: great stories that ooze with optimism seamlessly interwoven with important research findings that make mincemeat of the myth that the breakdown of marriage and relationships is inevitable. Most importantly Harry and Kate are super-practical about what to look for when you are looking for help. Read this whatever the State of your Union."

– Dr Samantha Callan, former advisor to David Cameron on Family and Society

"'I love you but you just don't seem interested in in me.' With those few words Kate and Harry Benson began a journey that eventually led to this book. Over many years I have found their story a true inspiration."

– Rob Parsons, OBE Author of *The Sixty Minute Father*

"*Many married men find themselves shocked and surprised when their wife tells them she wants a divorce a few years after kids come along. This scenario is provocatively and powerfully explained by this book. More importantly, Kate and Harry Benson explain how married fathers can renew their marriages when their wives are leaning towards leaving. Every dad should read this book.*"

– W Bradford Wilcox, Director of the National Marriage Project, University of Virginia and Senior Fellow, Institute for Family Studies

Previous books by Harry Benson:
Let's Stick Together: The relationship book for new parents (Lion Hudson, 2013)
Mentoring Marriages (Lion Hudson, 2005)
SCRAM! The gripping first hand account of the helicopter war in the Falklands (Preface)
Distinguished Service (Endeavour)

Previous books by Kate Benson:
Creative Steam Cuisine (Hamlyn, 1988)

WHAT MUMS WANT (AND DADS NEED TO KNOW)

HARRY AND KATE BENSON

LION

Text copyright © 2017 Harry and Kate Benson
This edition copyright © 2017 Lion Hudson

Published by Lion Books
an imprint of
Lion Hudson plc
Wilkinson House, Jordan Hill Road,
Oxford OX2 8DR, England
www.lionhudson.com/lion

ISBN 978 0 7459 6885 8
e-ISBN 978 0 7459 6886 5

First edition 2017

Acknowledgments

A catalogue record for this book is available from
the British Library

Printed and bound in Great Britain by
Marston Book Services Ltd, Oxfordshire

To our wise friends, without whom
we wouldn't have made it this far;
to our wonderful children who
make it all so worthwhile;
and to each other for ever and ever!

Contents

Foreword

I sometimes say, slightly light-heartedly, that I have been in the family breakdown business for more than eighty-five years: forty-five of them working at every level of the family justice system (barrister, QC, and High Court Family Judge) and forty-three being married to the same wife! This remark is made usually in the context of explaining why I felt driven to establish Marriage Foundation in 2012, having experienced both the pain and pleasure associated with marriage. It also explains the context in which I first met Harry, and later Kate, Benson. Because where they are concerned, I must start by "declaring an interest", for they have become over the course of the last five years good and close friends, and, in large measure this is through our shared passion to do something about the level of, and painful fall out from, family breakdown.

Our paths first crossed in a strange way. In 2009 Harry and I both took part (unaware of the other's existence) in a high quality BBC documentary about family breakdown produced by a serious journalist (John Ware). In fact, we never actually met during the production, but I saw Harry on the TV in the finished programme. At the time, he was running relationship education courses for the Bristol Family Community Trust. Having seen him on screen I knew immediately that he was the person who would be able to help me spearhead an organization dedicated to confronting and tackling this national tragedy by championing marriage as the primary antidote. Three years later, in 2012, and a few months before the launch of Marriage Foundation, I asked him if he would head up our research department. This was for the simple reason that there was literally no one else in the country with his depth and breadth of knowledge and understanding of both the theory and reality of family breakdown, its causes and cures. He accepted immediately (our initial and seminal discussion took place on mobile phones when he was in the Sainsbury's car park in Taunton where he had just completed the weekly shop, and I was in the Royal Courts of Justice in London during a break from a harrowing child abuse case).

Over the intervening period my confidence in his expertise and my respect for his profound and original take on this whole problem has increased exponentially. In my opinion and experience he remains the person who knows more about this business from every angle than anyone else around. His fertile mind never ceases to explore new angles and approaches. And much of the new and best research has been done via Marriage Foundation. But it is not just the theoretical causes which he has explored. Crucially, so far as this book is concerned, he and Kate have bravely made no secret of the fact that they have been to the very "brink" of family collapse and come back "older and wiser" and with six (sic) children.

There are dozens, if not hundreds, of books of advice about how to have and maintain a happy marriage. Almost none of them are written, as here, jointly by the two sides of the marriage and none of them combine huge resources of expert and original research with personal and painful experience.

Harry and Kate's book looks at the tough problems of long-term relationships straight in the eye, and in the end prescribes research-based but simple, age-old, tried-and-tested solutions. It is brutally honest. But when you have steeped yourself in their joint wisdom and experience you are left knowing you are in the presence of experts you can rely on and trust completely. That cannot be said about a number of the books in this area.

This book should be required (but entertaining) reading for everyone who is married (regardless of the state of their relationship) and anyone who aspires to a long-term and fulfilling relationship.

Sir Paul Coleridge, October 2016
Founder and chairman of Marriage Foundation

Acknowledgments

This book is for all the Harrys and Kates out there who needn't get into the mess that we did. We hope that telling our own "back from the brink" story will give couples realistic and practical hope that unhappy marriages can be turned around and that happy marriages can stay strong for life.

First of all, we want to thank the very special wise friends who were there in our moment of crisis, listening, never taking sides, encouraging us, and pointing us in the right direction. Without them we would never have got this far. Steve and Ali, John and Corinne, take a bow. You were there when we most needed you. Other wonderful couples were also hugely supportive when we were at our most vulnerable. Thank you to David and Lou, David and Ruth, Len and Jill, Greg and Cathy, Kurt and Hilary, Nicky and Sila. Today we still love sitting down with wise friends and having amazing conversations about marriage and relationships. Thank you especially to Arthur and Jenny, Thierry and Veronique. You have given us insights when we needed them and helped us move on when we were stuck. We love you.

But there is so much more to this book than just our own story. We have drawn on a wealth of serious research, including our own original survey of what mums want from dads, and talked to many other couples whose personal stories bring the whole thing to life.

So secondly, a big thank you to the amazing academics whose work adds to the body of knowledge of how families work. We've cited at least seventy studies in this book. Everybody has opinions on how families work. But it is research that separates the objective "wheat" from the subjective "chaff". More Harry's field than Kate's, there are a few researchers whose work stands out in the way they help make sense of what can often seem so confusing. We especially love the work of Professors Scott *@DecideOrSlide* Stanley, Paul Amato and Galena Rhoades, and have loved working personally with Professors Steve McKay and Spencer James.

Third, we've also loved hearing all of the personal stories. Thank you to all of you who trusted us. Your stories may be camouflaged to keep you anonymous but you are all very real and wonderful. Thank you also to the 291 mothers who took the time to answer our long online survey questionnaire. The results have allowed us to be really confident about what mums as a whole want from dads.

Fourth, we would like to thank former high court judge Sir Paul Coleridge for his Foreword, as well as for his friendship, support and wisdom over the past few years. Through the charity Marriage Foundation, he has fearlessly provided a much-needed national platform for marriage in the UK and for Harry's family research to inform a wider audience.

Fifth, we would also like to thank our publisher Lion Hudson. This is our third book with them and we are hugely grateful to Tony Collins for his longstanding and generous support, also to Leisa, Rhoda, Helen and Jenny for getting the book edited and out there.

And finally, we want to thank God who carries us and puts up with us and loves us no matter how much we blow it. Writing this book has reminded us how far we've come. We are still together and happily married by the skin of our teeth, there but for the grace of God... Can you imagine the alternative? Had we not been able to turn around our marriage, our older children Rosie and Polly would have been brought up by only one of us and might now have very different outlooks on life. Our other children Grace, Sizzle, Charlie and Johnnie wouldn't even exist. Kids, we love you!

Introduction

I hadn't the faintest idea what I was doing there.

It was a winter evening, and already dark. I'd gone straight from work to a church office. It was an odd place for me to go. Kate had been attending church on Sundays for the last year; I'd been a couple of times for our children's baptisms, but that was about it. I wasn't a religious type. More of an atheist, actually.

Kate was insistent that I come to a meeting with her and her vicar. Our girls, aged three and one, were being looked after at home.

The room was sparsely decorated. Kate and I sat next to each other on the plain sofa. Opposite sat the vicar, John, and his wife, Corinne. They were very warm and welcoming. But it felt as if we were in the spotlight, like sitting on a stage.

Corinne took the lead.

"Harry, do you have any idea what you're doing here?" She smiled at me.

"Not the foggiest," I replied.

"Then I think Kate ought to tell you the story."

Both of us turned to Kate, who looked startled, as if she'd been put on the spot like a rabbit in the headlights.

She looked at me and began speaking, hesitantly at first.

"You know I love you, Harry. I've always loved you."

I really had no idea where this was going. I waited for the "but".

"Since we've had the children," she continued, "I've found it harder and harder to talk to you. You provide us with a comfortable life. And you're wonderful with the girls when it suits you. But you don't seem at all interested in me."

I didn't know what to say. Kate paused as if thinking what to say next.

"Anyway, I met somebody who did show an interest in me. We've met a few times in a café. I think I've fallen for him. I'm really, really stuck. I know it's wrong and I don't know what to do."

She paused again. I felt numb. I glanced at the others, who said nothing. I turned back to Kate.

"Did you sleep with him?" I asked.

"No," she replied.

"Well, what's the problem?"

If I'd had the presence of mind to glance at John and Corinne again, I would have seen the look of shock on their faces. My lack of reaction to this bombshell told its own story.

I still felt numb. It wasn't to last.

"Anyway, Harry," Kate continued, "I've decided I can't go on like this for much longer. I married you because I loved you and wanted you to be my best friend. I knew you were closed but I thought things would change. This other man has shown me the kind of friendship I could be getting."

Kate paused before delivering the second bomb.

"You're not the friend I want and need. And if things don't change within the next year, then this marriage is over."

The white flash that shot through my head like a thunderbolt temporarily blinded me with a mixture of panic and terror.

I never saw it coming.

Whether she meant it literally or not didn't matter. What I heard was that I was on twelve months' notice. Then I would be out. My immediate thought was that I'd lose my children.

I utterly adored my two girls. Losing Kate would mean losing them. This thought shocked me to the core.

An hour earlier, I'd been at work, oblivious to the storm that awaited me. I enjoyed my job and was good at it. It more than paid our bills and gave us a comfortable life, free from worry.

Minutes earlier, I'd had a wife and children. Life was good.

Now I felt lost. In a flash it had all fallen apart.

The shock and surprise quickly gave way to confusion. It was my turn to be the rabbit in the headlights, frozen and unable to react. Kate was desperately unhappy; I had no idea how it had happened. I had no idea what I'd done wrong. I had even less idea what to do or say next.

Everyone accepts that good marriages can go bad. But it was never going to happen to us, was it?

It wasn't meant to be like this.

Dear mum

Women, you know your marriage is not all as it could be. I'm with you. You already have your hands full. So I'm not about to give you a list of extra things to do for your husband that will add to your daily burden. Most of this book is about affirming you as a woman and inviting your husband to put you first. I do, however, want to ask if you see your husband as part of your "care package". Because, even if he is the one who needs to make the change, your own mindset might not be doing you any favours.

When my husband is interested in me, and is kind and generous to me, every part of me lights up. I feel happier and more enthusiastic about everything. I feel more loving and physically more attracted to him. I have more energy. I'm more interested in him.

His attention makes me be me; it allows me to enjoy the relationship I always wanted. I can love, respect, honour, and adore. I can do things with and for my husband. That's the person I am. I don't have to put on a persona.

When my husband neglects me, I can put up with it for a bit. But it slowly weighs me down, like a wet blanket. It's demotivating, boring, unpleasant, and unsexy in the extreme. I feel cold and resentful. I don't even like the person that I love.

At these times, I tend to go into micro-manage mode. Life's negatives overwhelm all the positives, which means pointing out all the things that haven't been done, mended, or planned. It's as if they flash up in neon lights.

The wife who feels neglected talks about the bins, the children, the dishwasher, the bills, the mowing, the broken handle, the problem with the car, and the shopping. These are all the things that need doing.

What she really means is, "What about me?"

So doesn't it seem utterly ludicrous that we need to remind our husbands, the ones with whom we have our most intimate relationship on this planet, that we need them to notice us, to be friends with us, to be kind and gentle?

***

Harry's and my story is of a marriage brought back from the brink. It's a story that's both real and filled with hope. That's what I feel today after being married for thirty years. But the early years of our marriage seemed anything but hopeful, especially when we had young children. The confrontation you've just read about happened eight years into our married life. Far from the dream of "happily ever after", I languished in a state of utter dissatisfaction.

We should never have got into such a mess in the first place.

Harry's part in our downfall was mostly a matter of ignorance. My Harry hasn't a malicious bone in his body. For many years he was both a good man and a useless husband. He's still a good man. Now he's a lovely husband.

I played my part too. I need to hold my hands up and take some share of the responsibility for what went wrong in the first place. We'll come to that.

The supreme irony is that, as a couple whose marriage was in deep crisis, we have ended up teaching thousands of new parents and other couples how to have a happy marriage! The principles we have taught were well grounded in research into what works. But it was always encouraging to hear how many people could relate to our personal illustrations of the ups and downs of married life.

Yet even though our story strikes a chord with some couples, how representative is it of what you, or mums in general, might want?

Especially for this book, we surveyed 291 married mothers and asked them what they most wanted from their husband. Almost everybody told us the same three things:

We want him to be "a friend". This was the top-scoring factor out of a list of twenty-nine different roles, qualities, and characteristics. Almost every mother – 95 per cent – had "friendship" either at the top of their list or a close second.

We want him to be "interested in me". This was the single biggest difference between mums who were happy and those who weren't. Happy wives have husbands who put them high up on their list of priorities. Almost every wife – 97 per cent – had "interested in me" at or near the top of the list of what they thought was important.

We want him to be "interested in the children". Another big difference between happy and unhappy mums, almost everyone – 98 per cent – said children should be a top priority for their husband.

I was quite heartened by these findings. I wasn't the only mother who needed to feel cherished and enjoyed and loved. It seems that this is what most other mothers want as well.

For me, friendship means being kind and gentle. It means being prepared to drop stuff and listen, being open and encouraging with me, asking me how I am, being involved in my life, and being interested in my opinion. It means showing initiative and not waiting for me to ask. And it means noticing me and maybe giving the occasional compliment.

Just as important is what friendship isn't. It isn't loud, opinionated, and absolute. It isn't dismissive of things I do or like. It isn't about putting me down or belittling me. It isn't rude and disrespectful. It's also not about the functional side of life, how well we fulfil our different roles and responsibilities. It's definitely not about how well stuff gets fixed and money gets earned, and how well husbands provide – if that's how you choose to divide your roles.

Before we had children, we had time for each other and ourselves, energy, money, and flourishing careers. With those ingredients in the cupboard of life, it's not hard to enjoy this stage, even if the relationship has the odd flaw.

Becoming parents blew a hole in this idyll. We were supposed to be the happiest little family unit. We both wanted children, and our first daughter arrived at the perfect time, healthy and demanding. Two years later, our second was born.

As a new mother, I became completely wrapped up in my babies. I loved them to bursting and relished every moment of their newborn stage. "Milky heaven" is what I used to call that time. I didn't ever really think about what my having babies would do to my relationship with Harry.

Both of us got stuck into our new life as parents. I discovered that I was made to be a mother. Harry loved our girls instantly, and was a helpful and attentive father.

Our drifting apart was so very subtle. It wasn't all bleak, of course: we still had a lot of fun. But the inevitable post-baby exhaustion was thick and dark, like being in a long tunnel. I needed Harry to care about me and not just the baby. I couldn't put my finger on what I needed exactly, but I felt increasingly disappointed and cross that I wasn't getting it.

Harry sensed that he was in trouble and retreated somewhere inside himself that was safe and closed off. On the surface he was working hard to provide for us; he was emotionally engaged and engaging with our daughters. But our own cosy friendship seemed to slip away. At the same time, I pulled away from Harry to protect myself. I hid this conscious withdrawal behind the mammoth task of motherhood and the vortex it creates. We failed to check in with each other. We just functioned.

I know 100 per cent when I'm being noticed and cherished. I also know when I'm not.

When I asked Harry why it wasn't natural and automatic for him to be friendly and adore me, he said that he just didn't think about it. He would never be deliberately unfriendly or unkind. But, left to his own devices, it never crossed his mind that his number-one role was to be my friend, to adore me, to be pleased and interested in me, to be kind. Instead, he focused on work.

I wonder what I could have done better to make Harry know how much we loved and needed him.

Harry and other male friends have recently talked about being left out or cast aside the minute the baby came home. They felt cut out during pregnancy too, as our female brains, bodies, and emotions were already hooked on the baby. I simply didn't ever consider it at the time and, as Harry wasn't very emotionally literate, he never voiced it until much later.

For me, the turning points began with talking to a friend and led to the confrontation with Harry, about which you've just read.

For Harry, the turning points were the confrontation, which came like a bolt from the blue for him, and then a letter I wrote that made him change his whole attitude.

For our marriage, the turning points were all of these, followed by a marriage course we did over a weekend together. Thereafter it's been a question of working it out as we go along.

The changes Harry made were all very real, although it took ages for me to believe it. Harry still has all the qualities that I saw and loved in him when we got married thirty years ago. But the lack of friendship that plagued our early years together has now all but gone.

Our marriage today is scarcely recognizable from what it was then.

Harry puts the transformation of our marriage down to a one-way street. He describes it as the switch in his head that made him remember to be my friend and to treat me kindly. He did take responsibility for sorting out the mess. Both of us are all too aware that it hasn't been all plain sailing since then. But, over time, I've seen the changes and have come to trust that they are real. Our marriage has blossomed.

When a husband is kind and gentle to his wife, when he treats her as his friend, when he is thoughtful towards her and doesn't take her for granted, then she will respond.

When a husband loves his wife, then she will love him right back.

Is it sexist, or unfair, to say that things work best in this direction? Haven't times changed? Shouldn't it be up to both of us equally?

I really don't think so. Times may change; human nature doesn't. Men and women certainly have equal value and importance. But that doesn't mean we are the same.

The one fundamental and indisputable difference between men

and women is that women have babies and men don't. Whether it's to do with our genetic programming (which would therefore include adoptive mothers), or merely the mental conditioning of spending nine months pregnant, as mothers we tend to think about our children most or all of the time. Having a baby orients us towards our children and our home in a way that doesn't happen nearly as naturally for fathers.

The research we've looked at seems to show pretty clearly that the recipe for a happy family life is a happy wife. If the wife is happy, then so will the children and the husband be. It doesn't seem to be as true the other way round.

If our husbands want us to look up from our children and focus on them, then it's up to them to shine their light on us first. And when they do that ... aaaaahhhhhhhh! It's all that we want.

I sometimes think that the way I think about my children is the way I want Harry to think about me. I love my children. I want the best for them. I am aware of what's going on in their lives. I am interested in them. I encourage and support them. I notice them and listen to them. I spend time and money on them. I make space for them.

So does Harry, of course. But his love and attention to the children tend to come in bursts. Mine is a constant drip that is there in the background all the time.

I doubt whether Harry, or any husband, can sustain that kind of constant attention to his wife. But it's the attitude that counts. As long as I feel I'm high on his list of priorities, rather than an afterthought who is taken for granted, then life is good.

What could I have done differently?

When I became a mother, Harry became part of my child-and-home empire. Even if I wasn't getting my needs met, I should have treated him more like a husband and less like part of my "care package". It certainly didn't help. If I'd been more specific –

that I needed a friend, somebody who put me high on their list of priorities and then translated that attitude into actions – then we might have avoided our downward drift.

What we really needed was a book like this!

We hope you won't ever get into anything like the mess we did. But, if you already have, I know what it's like. I know what you're going through because I've been there myself. I've scraped the bottom of the marital barrel.

The whole point of this book is to help you both realize that you already have a rescuer. It's your husband.

Our message is that it is well within the capacity of any man, no matter how dire the state of his marriage, to be the husband his wife needs him to be.

You may have told him a thousand times yourself. But sometimes it takes another voice for him to hear it. That's our job.

This book is all about hope. It's for all you Harrys and Kates out there who needn't get into the mess we did.

Dear dad

Men, relax! This isn't another book telling you how to do relationships more like a woman. I want to show you how being a real man means being kind to your wife and showing that you care. That's it. It's not about being a doormat. It's about a simple mental shift that will end up getting you everything you ever wanted, and keep you out of trouble!

Every year, our family spend the first week of our summer holidays at a big Christian festival. I think of it as my annual "pruning" time after a busy year has come to an end. It's a time to relax with my family, let go of the pressures of work and other projects, and allow my mind to be cleared or "pruned" – in the same way that a grapevine is pruned after it has finished producing that year's bunches of fruit. The process of pruning clears away old unproductive branches and gives the vine the opportunity to grow fresh new branches that will fruit the following year. The analogy works for me, anyway.

So, by the time the week's camping has come to an end, I often have the first thoughts about how the following year might begin to take shape, as regards both work and family life. These are the very first shoots that suggest a direction of growth for the year ahead. I can then return to work in the autumn with an idea of what projects to pursue and what to drop, and where I need to focus at home.

Even if this time away only ever gives me clues about work, one subject has come up with regular clarity for many years. It is a reminder to be kind and gentle. Whenever I tell Kate this, she laughs, whether out of relief or exasperation.

"I've been telling you this for years, Harry," she says. "All I've ever needed is for you to be kind and gentle."

"Kind" sounds like such a namby-pamby word. But kindness lies at the heart of what mums want.

My friend Rob runs a successful medium-sized law firm. A few years ago, staff surveys told him that his firm was not a happy place to work. For months he and his staff tried to define the kind of ethos they would like instead. In the end, they reluctantly boiled it down to one word: nice.

"Nice" sounds like another namby-pamby word, doesn't it? "Just be nice." But it's what everyone at Rob's firm really wanted. The amazing thing is that when the people at the top of the firm made a point of being nice, to each other and to their staff, the whole atmosphere at work changed. Today Rob's firm has been voted twelfth out of the top 100 medium-sized firms in the country in which to work. It's a fantastic effort.

Nice. Kind. Gentle. These are the characteristics of a marriage that wives most crave and enjoy.

Today at our annual family camping holiday – and my annual season of "pruning" – I no longer hear a reminder to be kind any more. Other things spring to mind in its place.

Just as Rob's firm is now happy because it's "nice", my marriage is now happy because it's "kind". I have learned to be kind to my wife. It's what she wants. After that dreadful confrontation all those years ago, when Kate and I stood staring into the marital abyss, I can now say with confidence that we have a wonderfully happy marriage – as well as four more children!

***

Marriage, rather like parenting, doesn't come with a manual. Mostly, we have to figure it out for ourselves.

That's not so bad if we've been brought up by amazing parents who loved each other, had a secure marriage, and never let their differences come between them. And even if they didn't manage it themselves, our parents' friends may have had great marriages. Watching them gave us hope that great marriage is at least a possibility. It exists. It can work.

But what if we've never seen a great marriage at first hand? Maybe our parents split or fought or were barely ever a couple. Maybe most of our friends lived with only one parent. They'd never seen a great marriage either. Why should we believe something exists if we've never seen it?

I'm here to tell you that secure and happy marriage is an achievable reality that is within your reach. The secret is all in the mind.

Some of it undoubtedly boils down to knowing how to do it, knowing the practical skills of married life. The popular view is that it's all about communication. How to sit down and listen and really understand what your spouse is going through. How to weather the onslaught and not take it personally when she needs to let off steam. How to handle your inevitable differences, which means knowing when to sweep the less important issues under the carpet and how to resolve the important stuff together as a team. How to make her feel loved and special, even when you don't feel like it.

This is all stuff we can learn. How to get on well with your wife is a matter of how to communicate well.

But, on its own, communication will never be enough. Attitude is so much more important.

I can teach you all the communication skills in the world. But I also know from harsh experience that when I'm feeling defensive or unloved or upset or tired, none of it works.

What rescues me from plunging into the abyss is the big picture of how I see Kate. However much I may feel justifiably hurt, unfairly treated, put down, or whatever, I also want to spend the rest of my life with her. I certainly don't want her to be hurt. She's too special. And I trust that Kate loves me. So I don't let things get out of hand. I do eventually apologize. I stop being defensive. I let it go and eat humble pie.

It would be pretty dumb to win an argument and think I'd somehow retained the moral high ground, and yet lose Kate.

The best marriages are, of course, built on both great attitude and great skills. If you had to choose one of these, give me a couple who put each other first any day. They may be utterly dysfunctional in the way they communicate, but their attitude will see them through and keep them out of too much trouble.

Ultimately, the success of your marriage depends on your attitude to your wife. How do you see her? How important is she in your life? Where does she fit in the pecking order of your priorities?

Your work is undoubtedly important. Your children are important. Your hobbies and interests are important. But all of these are temporary compared to your marriage.

You'll probably change jobs or retire at some stage. Your

children will leave home (you hope!). Your interests will change over time.

Your marriage is for life. Your wife is for life. That was and is the plan. Sure, you and I both know that marriages don't always work out. But most do last for life.

What works is being kind and gentle with your wife.

The question I want to ask is, how do you treat your wife? That's the main theme of this book, the core of a successful marriage, and the key concern for wives. Where does she come on your list of priorities?

You'll know if work is at the top of that list because you're going to be willing to drop everything when work calls. It might be little things – you're tired but you'll answer that late-night email from your boss. But do you show that same kind of interest in your wife when she wants to tell you something about her day?

If you're not sure who is king in your life, ask your wife. She'll tell you because she notices.

Alternatively, your children may be at the top of your list of priorities. Maybe you'd rather spend money on a treat with the children than on taking your wife out for a romantic dinner. Or it may be hobbies: you just assume that you can go and play golf on Saturday. After all, it's fair enough after a hard week's work, isn't it? But is that what your wife wants? And, when she complains, does it seem as if she's out to destroy your fun?

When your wife comes first in your life, and knows she is first, she'll encourage you in your work because she knows it's important. She'll want to give you some freedom. There's an order to things. Once you've shown you'll do anything for her, you'll make sacrifices for her, she's bound to want to bless you so much. Who wouldn't?!

Love your wife. And she'll love you right back. In that order. This is the secret to a happy marriage.

In this book, I'm going to be talking about how you, as the husband, are the one who needs to take responsibility for your marriage. You may think it's unfair that you should take the lead on this. Equality is really important in the sense of your both having equal value. But equality doesn't work when it comes to responsibility.

Somebody has to carry the load, or nobody will. If you think both of you are equally responsible, I can pretty much guarantee that at some point your marriage will be at risk because both of you will expect the other to step up.

Shared responsibility ultimately means diminished responsibility.

Or perhaps you are worried that she might not respond. You do lots of nice things for her. But it's never enough. It reminds you of the popular song about a bloke who's willing to give everything up for his girl. But she wouldn't do the same, he complains.

Yeah, she would!

All I can say is try it for a while. Be kind and gentle to your wife. Put her interests first in your life. Be willing to drop everything, even at risk to your career or your children or your hobbies. And see what happens. What woman could resist a man who will do that?!

This will be easier than you think. You may not believe me yet. But your wife will. Humour me anyway and read on a little further!

In the rest of the book, I'll tell you how my own marriage got into such a mess, how we grew apart. Maybe it will ring some bells. Then I'll move on to why couples getting it wrong and splitting up matters anyway.

Half of all today's teenagers no longer live with both natural parents; family breakdown has become a norm. Alas, that doesn't mean it's OK. Having experienced it myself as child, I wanted Kate and me to stay together "for the sake of the kids". But that was never going to be enough.

It took a shocking letter from Kate to make me realize I needed to make our marriage work not for the kids but for her. That was the big turning point for me and for our marriage. After that awakening, we were in with a chance.

It was this tiny mental shift – putting my wife, and not my work or myself or anything else, first – that changed everything. This is what this book is about. This is all I'm suggesting you do. It'll make your wife happy: and a happy wife is the recipe for a happy family, according to a number of studies.

Happy wife, happy life. If our wives are happy, then the kids and husbands will be happy. It doesn't seem to work the other way round.

So what is it that wives want?

You'll be glad to know that I'm not just relying on what Kate or I think. For this book, we've conducted two new surveys and asked hundreds of women what they think. The number-one thing women say they want from their husband is friendship. That's it! A husband who is a friend to his wife.

That shouldn't be too hard. But for some it will be. Twenty years ago, I finally realized I needed to make it a priority to love my wife and be kind to her – rather than just be a good provider and a good dad. Eventually we went on a marriage course to learn how to do it. There I learned the practical skills that I mentioned earlier – how to be kind, how to listen, how to love her in a way that actually connects.

And so began a new episode of the married life we really ought to have had in the first place. The good times suddenly became better than ever. I felt more connected to Kate than ever. It began on the marriage weekend, when I fell in love with Kate in a way that I'd not experienced before. Ah!

Few, if any, marriages spend all their time on cloud nine. Everyone has downs as well as ups. We've had our fair share of shockers along the way. Some of them now make me laugh, but few of them did at the time.

A lot of this was down to ingrained bad habits. By this I mean the way we would have a misunderstanding and then head off down some negative path.

In the book, we'll introduce you to the idea of STOP signs: S – Scoring points, T – Thinking the worst, O – Opting out, P – Putting down. These are the top four bad habits that eventually wreck relationships.

Because all of us blow it from time to time, we all use STOP signs to some extent. The trick is to nip them in the bud early on before they start to become ingrained. I'm afraid you'll recognize yourself in one or more of these. I do. Kate does. Everyone does.

The bad habit that has taken me longest to bring under control is a toxic mixture of T and O – Thinking the worst and Opting out. If Kate asked me to do something for her, I'd often hear it as suggesting that I'd failed. It came across as a criticism. "Why haven't you done it, Harry? You've failed." Of course that's not what she said or even meant. But it's what I heard.

Thinking the worst meant I felt perpetually in trouble, unless shown otherwise. My response to being in trouble would then be to get defensive and close down, and even walk out for a while. Opting out then made it look as if I didn't care. Nobody feels put first if their spouse walks out like this.

Later on, I'll tell you how I finally found a way of overcoming this seemingly insidious problem a couple of years ago. I love this because it happened twenty-seven years into our marriage, illustrating how there is always something to learn about one another, something to do better.

A great marriage should never have to get stuck in a rut. If that's how it feels for you right now, I want to bring you hope. Our own story might do this for you. But we have others, each one from a fabulous real-life couple who have brought their marriage back from a seemingly impossible situation. We've camouflaged their details a little for privacy. But these are people we know who have shown that it's not over until it's over. There's always hope.

A common theme for them and us is the support of wise friends along the way. Not all friends are wise – some can be downright foolish. But you'll know those around you who are wise. Talk to them.

A variety of friends supported us along the way, some challenging us, some encouraging, some giving practical advice. We'll talk about how to spot wise friends and how to be that friend for somebody else.

***

This book is not mere "pop psychology".

What we have to say about marriage and family life is rooted in the findings of some seventy academic studies. These are referenced in the notes and involve thousands and thousands of couples and families from the UK, the US, and around the world. The stories that we tell – our own and other couples' – are there to bring life to this research into what works.

The answer to what mums want is not a diamond ring. They might tell you that in public. But, in private, they will tell you what they really want is a man who cares for them, who treats them as special, who cherishes them, who is kind and gentle and considerate. They want a friend.

In the end, it's not about how well you provide for your family. After all, the giant leap in equality of opportunity now means that women can do that perfectly well for themselves. And, as I remember once hearing from the family author Rob Parsons, nobody ever went to their grave saying "I wish I'd spent more time at the office."

Great marriage is based on attitude, on how you treat one another, on being kind.

Are you a real man? Sure you are. A real man is one who loves his wife. And when he does, she loves him right back.

This is the book Kate and I would like to have read when we got married. It just might have prevented our early descent into misery and, instead, nudged us towards the kind of wonderfully happy marriage that we always wanted and now have.

Nobody says marriage is easy. Ours hasn't always been plain sailing. That's real life. But our marriage today is totally unrecognizable from what it was at that meeting.

May you be the real man your wife needs you to be, may you love your wife, and may your marriage flourish as a result.

It wasn't meant to be like this...

"I never saw it coming," said Harry. "You're not the friend I want and need," Kate told him. "And if things don't change within the next year, then this marriage will be over." Harry and Kate share their story of how their eight-year marriage, with two young children, went so wrong.

I first met Harry at a party when I was nineteen, almost twenty.

There was something about Harry that made me connect with him immediately. He ticked so many boxes. He was kind, genuine, and honourable. I picked up those traits very quickly. We had similar social backgrounds, which mattered because of the way I'd been brought up.

He was obviously highly capable in his job as a Navy helicopter pilot. But he was also fiercely independent. This made him awkward at times and not especially good with people. He was never rude; he just didn't seem to need anybody. Paradoxically, this made me feel safe. It meant he wasn't going to run off with anybody else.

When we started going out we had some really big ups. We

had a lot of fun together. But we also had some really, really big downs.

Adding a girlfriend to the mix didn't seem to change him. He didn't appear to care too much about me or put himself out for me. He was very much his own man. It wasn't as if he was doing it for anybody else either. He was just Harry being Harry.

Despite this, Harry's good traits comfortably outnumbered the bad. I made up my mind quite early on that he was the one for me. It was less about being head over heels in love and more about thinking that I'd be safe. All I needed was for him to make me happy.

It was quite a shock when he asked me to marry him, as I still didn't feel I was that special to him. But it didn't put me off; it just triggered my fighting instinct: "I will get him," I thought. "I'll conquer him. I'll make him care about me."

I was determined. I thought I could sort him out!

Our wedding day was utterly glorious: a classic rural English wedding on a beautiful sunny day.

I arrived at the church feeling excited and not a bit frightened. I am the sort of person who will leap out of a plane because I've made a decision to do it. So I leapt up the aisle saying, "I've decided to do this."

Our perfect day ended with the huge surprise of being flown away in a helicopter. I love surprises.

As I flew away after making my vows, it never occurred to me that we wouldn't be together for ever and ever. I was thrilled to be his wife.

Even if he had some rough edges, I knew I'd married a good man. I'd chosen someone who could look after me. That didn't mean I would be a floppy wife – I had my own ambitions. But it was enough that Harry was never going to be a layabout or a loser. He was intelligent and ambitious and wanted to get on.

All he needed was a bit of training on how to look after a girl, how to listen, how to understand. That probably sounds awful but I just assumed things were going to work out. Failure never crossed my mind.

"We'll sort it out," I thought.

***

Our wedding was indeed on the most beautiful English summer's day imaginable. We got married in a tiny church up a quiet and leafy country lane.

The word "quintessential" was invented for such an occasion. In every possible way, it was a quintessentially English wedding, straight out of the pages of Jane Austen.

Twenty-five years old, I wore my dark blue naval uniform, pilot's wings on my sleeve, Falklands War medal pinned to my lapel next to a white rose.

As I stood nervously at the head of the aisle waiting for my beautiful bride, I passed the wedding ring across to my best man for safe keeping.

"Harry." My five-times-married aunt leant over to me holding out her own hand, fingers outstretched.

"If you lose the ring," she whispered mischievously, "I've got five more you can borrow!"

I laughed. Five weddings! The thought was absurd. One wedding was all I would ever need.

I didn't watch Kate walk up the aisle behind me because somebody had told me beforehand that it was bad luck. Instead, I stood rigidly facing forward as the bridal music played. I wanted to do the right thing.

Then my bride appeared magically next to me, looking stunning in a flowing white dress topped with a frilled collar in the 1980s style.

Her veil lifted, to reveal the pretty, smiling face of the young woman I was about to marry. Kate.

We said our vows.

"For better, for worse.

For richer, for poorer.

In sickness and in health.

To love and to cherish.

Till death us do part."

Duly pronounced man and wife, we walked slowly back down the aisle, hanging on to each other's hand, grinning madly at friends and family.

Outside the church, dappled sunlight filtered down through the canopy of oak and ash trees that shaded us. Eight military friends, mostly fellow pilots from the Royal Navy, stood smartly to attention and held up their ceremonial swords in an arch above our heads.

In that moment, all was well with the world. Our marriage could only be "for better, for richer, in health".

Had somebody told me that we would stand on the brink of divorce just eight years later, I would have scoffed at them and suggested they had had too much to drink.

Just as the idea of getting married five times was absurd, so too was "for worse, for poorer, in sickness".

Even if somebody had emphasized the importance of these vows to me at the time, I would have nodded politely. But I wouldn't have heard a word.

"Harry," they might have said, "the whole point of getting married is to make it crystal clear to everyone that you'll stick it out no matter what, even in the bad times when things aren't so rosy."

That was all very well. But bad times weren't going to happen to us. Were they?

***

Soon after we got married, Harry left the Navy for a job in business, and we moved overseas.

As a young married woman, I had a really nice, comfortable life. Harry took a pay cut because of the career change. But we still had a good lifestyle, with lots of friends. I built up my small cookery business, eventually moving on to edit a foodie magazine. Harry was always supportive of what I did. As his new career took off, we moved up in the world from living in a small flat to a house with a garden.

On the outside, we probably looked pretty good as a couple. We did all the right things together, socializing, eating out, looking good, having fun. At home we functioned well as a team. He did the bins. I did the shopping. That sort of thing.

But, under the surface, things didn't change.

When Harry had been away at sea, it was obviously hard for him to keep in touch with me. Then he came back for a day or two and still didn't call me. I'd felt so disappointed. If I wasn't in front of his eyes, he didn't seem to think about me at all. At least then I knew he was exhausted and had only short breaks. It didn't feel as if he was putting me first, but there was a reason.

I assumed things would change when we got married. We would spend more time together. My husband would put me first. Why wouldn't he?! He'd be interested in me and my life. We'd chat together at home and, when we were at work, he'd call me to see how I was. It didn't happen.

Instead, we drifted slowly apart. We became more like flatmates or strangers behind closed doors.

Harry seemed more comfortable sitting down with a newspaper than asking about me, my day, my work. When we did talk, it was mostly about his work. I felt he wasn't interested in me. It was obvious who came first in his life and it wasn't me. I became increasingly lonely.

To be fair, I needed Harry to make me happy. He didn't know how to do that. It never occurred to me that I needed to take responsibility for my own happiness. Nor did I realize at the time that I was also struggling with mild anxiety and depression. I needed somebody to make me feel better. When Harry didn't show the interest I needed, I would believe it was because I didn't have much to say. So then I wouldn't say anything. He in turn wouldn't show any interest. It was a self-perpetuating cycle of gloom.

My radar was set to see things as either really good or really bad. Whatever Harry did would show either that he loved me or that he didn't: the time he gave me, how he spoke to me, the way we talked, what we did when we went out. It was a black-and-white thing, good or bad, with not much in between. And when I did judge things to be bad, I would become more and more disappointed, more and more critical.

The funny thing is that I could have fun with my friends and invite people over. Harry might or might not enjoy it. He never made a fuss about what we did. He either entered in or didn't. I never quite knew what would make him enjoy something or not.

I wanted to blame Harry for being so closed and unemotional. As my husband, he certainly should have taken a basic responsibility for showing an interest in me, for spending time with me, for looking after me, for caring for me, for being my friend. He didn't. On the other hand, I don't suppose I spelled it out quite as clearly as that.

As my expectations were dashed, I gradually closed down. I don't think he noticed. Still, it wasn't very nice for him. From his point of view, whatever he did as my provider seemed to count for nothing. He felt unable to make me happy. Nothing would ever be enough.

Of course I tried telling him, "I just need you to be my friend." But that just confused him and he could never understand what I meant.

I'd planned to teach him how to be with me. But I never really did.

Then I got pregnant with our first child. Because our life was so comfortable on the outside, in some ways becoming parents was perfect. But there was a real emptiness in our relationship. It's as if the building was in place. But there was nothing inside.

I loved being a mother. I felt secure and safe. Harry encouraged me to do whatever I wanted as a mum. He was a really involved father. I was actually quite impressed! The only area I wouldn't let him near was feeding. That was my treat, and I was territorial about it. But, otherwise, he was very sweet with his new daughter and happy to get stuck in to being a dad. He loved her very much.

Yet, as husband and wife, we still had this kind of nothing-y relationship. Harry remained incredibly protective of his own time and space, so that he could do the things he wanted to do. When we did talk, instead of talking about his work (which was all we had talked about before), now we replaced it with talking about our daughter.

Meanwhile, my mild anxiety and depression continued.

When I was down, I did try to explain what I needed. I often thought to myself, "This isn't working, Harry. What's in it for me, Harry? What are you going to do to make me happy, Harry?"

I told him I wanted him to take time with me, be interested in me, do things with me, talk to me. I thought I was being very clear. But he didn't ever quite know what I meant. I think it just sounded confusing to him.

***

It's so easy to be consumed by circumstances.

When you're in a good place, life is good, the sun is shining, and the world seems bright and rosy. Bad times are out of sight and out of mind. Not only do you not think about them, you can't think about them.

That's how I felt when I married Kate. And that's how Kate felt when she married me. Our wedding day was so full of fun and happiness and love and exuberance. Problems simply never crossed our minds. Bad things happened to other people.

It was a day of affirmation. Happily ever after had begun.

So how on earth did it go so wrong?

Frankly, I never noticed the drift.

The road ahead seemed pretty straightforward. I had married Kate and wanted to do the best for her. That meant making my career work. Everything in me said that a man's job was to provide. So that's what I did.

Soon after our wedding, I left the Navy in search of a career in business and the prospect of a life abroad for both of us. I got stuck in to my new work. Even though the pay was lower, I could see the upside. The first few years would be my apprenticeship.

Being sent overseas told me that we were on the right track. Our quality of life started to pick up. After starting her own catering business, Kate managed to get a job with a cookery magazine. I was very proud of her. During the week, we had an active social life, with lots of new friends. At weekends, we tried to travel as much as possible. Life was good.

Having learned something of my new trade, I changed companies in order to take on more responsibility and climb a little further up the ladder. We moved country again just at the time Kate became pregnant. Both of us decided a move was the right thing to do. I was as excited about my new job in a new country as about becoming a father for the first time.

The only cloud on the horizon was that every so often Kate and I would have a misunderstanding about something. Invariably, these ended in a frosty silence. Kate was cross with me and I was confused. I could never completely understand what I'd done to make her so upset.

I resolved to make sure I did the best I possibly could in my new job. That would give us the life we both wanted.

When our first daughter was born, I fell hopelessly in love. I got stuck in to the role of being a father. Bathtime, changing nappies, cleaning eyes: you name it. I loved being a father. Kate also loved being a mother and was naturally brilliant at it.

As new parents, our happy social life somehow continued. Being the first to have a baby among our overseas friends gave us a certain novelty value and cachet. A year and a half later, Kate was pregnant again with our second. Life really was good.

Almost as soon as we found this out, I was summoned to headquarters to meet my new big boss. Just months earlier, the previous boss had told me I was doing well, so much so that he had given me a pay rise. To my considerable shock and surprise, the new boss thought otherwise. Despite our being very happy where we were, he wanted me to move country once more, against my wishes. Worse, my new role brought another big pay cut into the bargain.

With Kate newly pregnant and our first child only just learning to walk, I couldn't tell the new boss to get stuffed. I was vulnerable at home. I had to protect my family and wasn't yet sufficiently confident to risk leaving my job. My only choice was to accept the new role. It wasn't what either of us wanted. I felt stuck and thoroughly depressed, torn between my instincts for "fight or flight".

Reluctantly, we moved. Our gorgeous second daughter was born. But the cloud over my head at work meant I took my eye off the ball at home. After a few months of fighting to make a name for myself, I was offered an exciting new job with a small partnership, and took great pleasure in handing in my notice.

I had to make it work for my family.

***

Harry loved our daughters but was very quick – or so it seemed to me – to take a position of diminished responsibility at home.

When he wasn't working, he was happy to do whatever I asked him to do. To that extent, he was helpful. But it meant he didn't take things off my shoulders unless I made it happen. I was still carrying the load.

Often it felt as if I was asking for favours: "Please would you hang the washing up? Please would you cook supper tonight? Please could you go and put the children to bed? Please would you change that nappy? Please could you put the potatoes on?"

He would always do what I asked, even if it sometimes felt irksome to him. It made me sound like a scratched record. Anyway, I thought, why should I be constantly in charge of the routine and everything?

I used to dread Saturdays in particular.

Somewhere in my belief system, I thought Saturday might be a day when Harry could shine a bit of light on me. Perhaps he might treat me a bit more specially, or take the children off my hands so that I could have a little bit of a rest, or whatever.

Instead, it seemed like any other day but with the addition of having an extra child in the house, off duty unless begged to help. Instead of Harry looking after me, I had to look after him. It felt doubly disappointing.

It also didn't help that I wanted to get out of the house and do something different on Saturdays. I'd been cooped up with the children all week. Being at home meant constantly thinking about the mess and the next meal. I couldn't ever totally relax. So I wanted to get out.

Harry, on the other hand, had been cooped up in an office all week and wanted to rest at home. Any plan I had to go for a walk or to take the girls swimming meant dragging him out of whatever chair he'd plonked himself in and then dealing with a reluctant passenger for the rest of the trip.

I just needed him to lift some of the load from me and take charge. I needed him to be kind to me. Instead, it was a double negative. I felt frustrated and undervalued. In his life, I was anywhere but first.

***

Our slow drift apart only really became apparent to me when we had time on our own. During the week, I could hide behind the busyness of work and our daily routines. But, at weekends or on holiday, with or without the children, our inability to communicate produced times of uncomfortable tension.

A particularly low point was a few days that we spent away in a beautiful beach hut. We had arranged for the children to be looked after at home while we jetted off.

The beach resort was like paradise. The sun shone. The sea was warm and sparkling. The local food was delicious. Without children, we had freedom to chat, walk, swim, read, or do nothing. It should have been a magical time.

Yet, instead of relaxing, I spent the entire time on tenterhooks, never quite understanding why Kate wasn't happy, never quite knowing what to say.

Several times I asked Kate what was wrong. Several times she tried to tell me. But we failed to connect. Mutually frustrated, we spent the days together but alone.

***

I think by now I had resigned myself to a lifeless marriage. We'd been married for nearly eight years. I was drifting further and further away from Harry emotionally. I wasn't getting what I needed from him. He wasn't spending time on me. Nor was he particularly focused on the kids. He would do the things I asked him to do. But he wouldn't initiate anything for me or the children.

Over time, I got more and more fed up. I noticed more and more ways in which he was falling short. I was respecting him less and less. I was interested in him less and less. I didn't want to hear about his work. I was cross, but at the same time I wasn't going to do anything about it, or so I thought.

Something needed to happen – a catalyst – to take us to the tipping point.

I started to run a mothers and toddlers group at our local church. More than anything, I did it because I thought it would be nice for my own children. The church's youth minister was incredibly helpful and supportive in getting it set up.

Absolutely shockingly, because I was neither expecting it nor looking for it, I found myself developing the most extreme crush on him. He was spending time chatting with me. He was teaching me stuff. He even made compilations of songs and music that showed he was thinking about me, Kate.

It was all the things I'd ever wanted from Harry but had never had. Harry seemed uninterested and withdrawn most of the time. This other bloke noticed me and made me feel special. It was as if he was shining a light on me. I felt as though I was interesting. I even felt pretty; I wasn't just the bag lady at home.

I began to believe, with complete certainty, that I'd be so much better off with him. He knew how to make me happy. He told me what a great mother I was, that I was beautiful and intelligent, that I had leadership skills, and that I was an asset to his team.

I also knew that it wasn't right. I was married with young children, as was he. But I was stuck.

At home one night, I told Harry I was falling for this guy. It was yet another shock when Harry didn't react in the slightest. "There you are then," I thought. "He doesn't even care." Nothing was going to change unless I did something about it. I felt so alone.

I went to the vicar, John, and asked for help. He helped me set up some sensible boundaries to stop this crush on the other man turning into something more serious. But ultimately I needed Harry to love me himself.

So we set up the meeting with John and his wife, Corinne, and Harry. Harry had no idea what was coming. When I reminded him about the other guy, his lack of reaction confirmed all my worst fears.

Harry didn't react at all. He wasn't angry. He wasn't sad. He just looked blank. He asked if I had slept with him. I hadn't.

"Well, what's the problem, then?"

It was horrible. I was stuck with a man who didn't give a hoot, didn't understand, didn't care about me at all. I was caught between a rock and a hard place. Life was so unfair. I had a chance to be happy and couldn't take it.

Our marriage was as dry as old bones. There was no hope. I couldn't get Harry to understand what I needed. I couldn't imagine that it would ever change.

I gave Harry a year. It wasn't meant to be like this.

For the sake of the children?

Family breakdown is at epidemic levels. Growing apart has overtaken adultery as the number-one cause. The result? Half of our teens don't live with both their natural parents. But it's not the high-conflict break-ups that tend to cause the most damage. It's the low-conflict ones, where children don't see it coming. In the case of Judith, her parents' sudden divorce still affects her decades later. Should parents stay together for the sake of the kids? The choice seems to be a life of misery instead of a life of freedom. But it's a false choice. Six months on from their confrontation, a letter from Kate finally shocked Harry into realizing he needed to make his marriage work for the sake of his wife, not their kids.

Judith told us that her childhood had been idyllic.

Together with her parents and her brother, Robert, she lived on the suburban outskirts of a major city in the north of England. Throughout her upbringing, Judith felt loved by her parents. They were not shy in showing their affection for each other or for their children, hugging her regularly, often telling her she was loved, and comforting her without hesitation or judgment when she needed support.

For as long as she could remember, they had always been there. It had never occurred to her to worry about whether she would be fed, or picked up from school, or supported in her exams. The love she got from her parents was reliable.

The family did a lot together as a unit. There were Christmas and birthday traditions, as well as shared family holidays in the summer, often at the same cottage deep in the English countryside. Mealtime with laughter was the centrepiece of everyday family life. Mum was a good home cook; Dad was funny. Judith's parents were affectionate to each other in a way that often prompted her and Robert to protest, "Oh Mum, Dad, do you have to?" Secretly she loved it when she watched them being tender towards one another. The atmosphere at home was warm and loving and it made Judith feel secure.

Judith was eighteen and had just finished her final school exams when the family sat down for what she assumed would be just another normal meal.

Her father spread his hands out on the table.

"Judith and Robert," he announced, with uncharacteristic seriousness.

"I've fallen in love with another woman. I'll be moving out this weekend."

Judith never saw it coming. The shock was tangible. She couldn't believe that all their years together, all the fondness and the love they had shown for one another, were going to be swept away, just like that.

Soon after her father had moved out and while they were still digesting the shock of it all, Judith's mother told her that they had been having problems for many years. They'd tried to work it out, but their conversations, always behind closed doors and out of sight and hearing of the children, had invariably broken down into bickering and argument. Both parents had felt hurt and closed. Yet somehow they had maintained an act of apparent unity in front of the children.

Finally, they had agreed that separation would be in the best interests of the children, although there was no clear plan for how or when this might actually happen.

It was months later that Judith's father confessed to her mother that he had been seeing somebody else. Although this was a huge shock, her mother said she was able to view it as a symptom of their problems, rather than the cause. Nonetheless, revelation of the affair acted as a catalyst for their split. The dinner with Judith and Robert came a few days later.

After leaving home, Judith trained as a nurse and blossomed into a beautiful young woman. Although her father remarried, on the few occasions when she saw her parents together they seemed to get on as if nothing had happened. The pretence was weird.

During her twenties, Judith had no shortage of admirers and was approached by several potential suitors. Eventually she fell in love.

John loved her enough to move across country and change jobs in order to be with her. Over the next four years, he asked her to marry him on several occasions. Each time she said no. She wasn't sure he was the one. Actually, more to the point, she was scared of saying yes. Her reaction was automatic and subconscious. The prospect of her own marriage going wrong and ending in divorce – just as her parents' had done – was too big a risk to take.

Eventually, John's perseverance ran out. He gave up on Judith and left to pursue his burgeoning career. Judith was heartbroken, as was John.

There were no more men in her life until Paul arrived five years later. Now Judith was in her mid-thirties, thoughts of children and marriage played ever more on her mind.

Although she loved Paul, her relationship with him was never quite what she'd hoped for. Their conversations were fraught with communication difficulties that escalated quickly into nasty rows. Any time she made a request of him, let alone a suggestion, he would accuse her of being critical and hard to please.

They drifted on for several years, splitting up and getting back together twice along the way. Part of her hoped he would ask her to marry him. Part of her hoped he wouldn't. She wasn't sure if she could commit her life to a relationship like this.

On her fortieth birthday, Judith realized that she had blown her big chance. She should have married John. He had fought for her; he had proved it by moving jobs and asking her to marry him several times. She had loved him. He had been the one. Now it was too late.

She began to realize how her parents' sudden break-up had shattered her trust in relationships. She was in a fog. It had turned her into a commitment-phobe.

She told Paul it was over.

***

There's an old joke about how to boil a frog. If you tried to drop a frog into a pot of hot water, it would jump straight out. But if you start it in cold water and very slowly raise the temperature – apparently – the frog doesn't notice the danger until it is too late.

The real joke is that it's about us. We're the boiled frogs.

Epidemic levels of family breakdown have crept up on us unawares. In the UK today, one-quarter of our two-year-olds and nearly half of all teenagers are not living with both natural parents.[1]

We asked our two youngest children, both teenagers, about their own school classes. One said the figure was less than half. The other said more than half. He could even give us an exact number of those living only with their mum. How did he know who they were? Obvious, he said. They are the annoying ones.

This is a shocking state of affairs, not least because as adults we seem so untroubled by the sheer scale of family breakdown. Yet the evidence is all around if we choose to see it.

Ask the teachers in the classrooms. They'll tell you about little Sammy who turned into a thorough nuisance after his dad left home. Or little Alice who would be doing so much better at school if she wasn't piggy in the middle between her warring parents.

Ask the doctors faced by a deluge of teenage mental health problems, many of which are the direct result of identity issues. Their mixed-up family lives leave them not knowing where they come from or who they are.

Ask the judges who see a stream of human misery pass through the family courts. Bitter and distressed couples take it out on each other at the expense of their children.

Ask the children themselves.

In the UK, we now spend more on family breakdown than we do on defence.[2] It equates to about half of what we spend on education. Most of the money goes on welfare support, such as housing and benefits, for lone parents. The rest goes on dealing with the health and safety needs of dysfunctional couples.

Yet, unlike defence or education, there's no government minister or department to take responsibility for family breakdown. And there's virtually no attempt to decide whether anything can be done about it or whether it is simply inevitable.

Imagine you live in a street with eight houses, each of which houses a family with children. If you and your neighbours are typical of Britain as a whole, then five of you will be married families, two will be lone-parent families, and one will be a cohabiting couple.

Had you lived in the same street thirty years ago, seven of you would have been married families and one a lone-parent family. There would have been no cohabiting couples.

The big change has been the emergence of cohabitation, which barely existed before the 1970s, when birth control became widely available. Now, of course, it is commonplace. The downside of this increase in less formal relationships has been a doubling of family breakdown – even though divorce rates are now much lower than they were thirty years ago.

It's a simple equation. Couples who marry are a lot more likely to stay together than those who don't marry.[3] So fewer couples marrying means more couples splitting up. The trend away from marriage is what's driving family breakdown.

To the extent that we think about family breakdown at all – other than wrongly blaming high divorce rates – we tend to think about it from an adult perspective.

Nobody, barring extreme conservatives, seriously thinks two adults should stay together in perpetuity if they are deeply unhappy. And so we have given birth to the famous rhetorical question:

"Should we stay together for the sake of the children?"

The answer seems self-evident to any right-thinking person. Instead of staying trapped in permanent misery, get out and be free to start again. Everybody will be a lot happier that way, adults and children alike. Won't they?

The only problem is that the assumptions behind this question are all wrong.

For starters, staying together doesn't have to mean being resigned to a hopelessly unhappy marriage for ever. For most of us, times of happiness and unhappiness come and go. People change. Circumstances change.

A large-scale American study conducted in the late 1980s and early 1990s by Professor Linda Waite from the University of Chicago found that two-thirds of those who stayed together after reporting being unhappy in their marriage said they were happily married five years later.[4]

For most people, staying together in what seemed like an unhappy marriage actually worked out pretty well. That's a rather astonishing turnaround.

In a follow-up study, Professor Waite asked some of the couples how they did it. They gave three main reasons.

In some cases, circumstances changed and a bad situation improved.

In others, unhappy people changed their own lives in ways that made them happier.

And, in others still, couples made a decision to make their marriage work.

In a more up-to-date UK study for Marriage Foundation, Harry and Professor Stephen McKay of the University of Lincoln looked at a big ongoing survey of mothers with eleven-year-old children, who were still living with the child's father.[5]

The results were remarkably similar. Out of the tiny minority of mums who had been unhappy with their relationship when their baby was born, most now said they were happy. Even more amazing is that, of the mums who had been unhappiest, half now said they were very happy.

Ten years may be a long time but this still looks like a pretty remarkable turnaround.

Curiously, the couples who were most likely to have split up during this time weren't the unhappiest ones or those who thought they were closest to the brink. These couples did just as well as the happiest and least worried ones. Remarkably, it was the ones in the middle, those who were neither especially happy nor unhappy, neither especially worried nor secure, who did worst.

As if to rub it in, half of the mothers we surveyed for this book who said they were now "happy with their relationship" had, at some point in the past, been "unhappy". One-quarter had been "very unhappy".[6]

Staying together in an unhappy marriage, whether it's for the sake of the children or for anyone else, seems to prove worthwhile for the majority.

All in all, US and UK evidence completely undermines the idea that unhappiness is permanent and therefore an unhappy marriage is necessarily best ended. This isn't to deny the reality that some marriages or relationships are truly unpleasant and everybody would be better off out. It's just that most aren't.

If you are unhappy now, the chances are that things will improve if you stick at it. Either your circumstances will change, or you will change your attitude to life, or you will make a decision to work on your marriage. We'll have more to say on the subject of happiness in a later chapter.

What happens when families do split up?

Parental resources take an immediate hit. Whereas before there were two pairs of hands to run the home, look after the children, and earn enough money to pay for it all, now there are two homes with only one pair of hands in each. If earnings don't change, only the better-off families can make this transition and still manage to pay all the extra bills.

For most families, therefore, money becomes a problem and everybody has to downsize. A collapse into poverty becomes a real possibility. In the UK, lone parents are seven times more likely to be in the lowest income group than couples with children.[7]

Because the resident parent now has to run the home single-handedly, without support at hand there's less time for eating or reading or playing with children. Input from the non-resident parent, usually the father, is bound to reduce. Indeed, having moved away, some fathers lose contact altogether. Many lone parents overcompensate for this by being either too lax or too strict in their parenting.[8]

Moving home, problems with money, lack of paternal involvement, and poor parenting all have negative consequences for children. A veritable sea of research links family breakdown with children's outcomes. Very roughly, one in ten children who do live with both natural parents also experience some kind of serious problem in their life – whether emotional or behavioural problems, poorer exam results, or later problems with relationships as an adult. That goes up to one in four among children whose parents have separated.[9]

Whether this is a big deal or not depends on your perspective.

The relaxed view is that the vast majority of children do fine regardless of family breakdown. The average extent to which children are disadvantaged when parents split up tends to be fairly small.

The concerned view is that family breakdown more than doubles the chances of such problems. Small reductions in well-being can have a big impact on children's later lives. And, even if there are cases where everybody is better off out, the overall findings from virtually every study are negative.[10]

It's tempting to look at family breakdown from the perspective of how the process is managed after divorce or separation has taken place. Make it all amicable, support lone parents, get dads involved, and you can have a "good divorce".

Unfortunately, there's little evidence that the so-called "good divorce" is actually good for children. Sure, adults feel a whole lot better if they aren't at each other's throats, are co-operating together as co-parents, and can settle the arrangements amicably – like grown-ups.

US sociologist Professor Paul Amato of Pennsylvania State University has probably studied the effects of divorce on children more than anyone. In one of his studies, he compared teenagers and young adults whose parents were co-operative – the "good divorce" – with those whose parents were unco-operative and those where one parent was doing it all on their own.[11]

The "good-divorce" children did better in two ways. According to their parents, they behaved better and got on better with their dad. But in terms of how happy they were in themselves, how satisfied they were with life overall, how well they did at school, and whether or not they used drugs, they did no better or worse than those with no input from the non-resident parent. Much the same was true for young adults whose parents had gone through a "good divorce". There were no subsequent differences at all in drug use or sexual or relational behaviour.

In a way, this is good news for lone parents who are genuinely left holding the baby – or child or young adult – on their own. They're no more disadvantaged than those who think they can "consciously uncouple" – the peculiar expression popularized by a celebrity couple – and not leave any scars on their children.

It's bad news, however, for advocates of the "good divorce", which turns out to be largely a myth.

This brings us to another factor at play here. What happens before the divorce or separation is more important than anything that happens afterwards.

Other studies by Professor Amato – with his colleague Professor Alan Booth – have followed families in real time, asking parents every few years about the quality and status of their relationship, how happy they are, and how often they argue, and finding out how the children are getting on. Because some of these parents then split up, the professors could compare how the children got on before and after the split.[12]

It turns out that the level of conflict between the parents while they were still together radically influences the way children respond to their parents' break-up.

Where conflict was high, and the relationship was clearly a

disaster, children were better off out of it. Their relationships with peers and family, their well-being, their behaviour, and their school performance all seemed to benefit in the first few years after the separation.

This makes a great deal of sense. Children struggle in a household full of conflict, stress, and fear. Freed from this toxic environment, they thrive in spite of any reduction in circumstances.

Where conflict was low, the parents seemed to be getting on fine, and the children were thriving, divorce or separation came out of the blue – as it did for Judith. The children may have had indications of the friction or iciness between their parents. But, with nothing terribly obvious, the split was a huge surprise. "Mummy and Daddy don't love each other any more" makes absolutely no sense. These children tended to do a lot worse after the split.

Furthermore, the only way to rationalize the break-up is to assume either that relationships just go pop for no apparent reason, or that "It was my fault. I caused it." Either interpretation is likely to sabotage a child's own relationships when he or she becomes an adult.

Why trust, why commit, when it will all end in tears without warning?

Somehow, we have come to believe that what happens after the divorce is the really important bit. That may be true for the adults, but it's a lot less true for the children. Children need to see why things went wrong. What happened before the divorce sets the scene and is arguably more important for them.

The terrible tragedy is that the vast majority of family breakdown comes out of these "low-conflict" relationships.

Another study Harry did for Marriage Foundation – this time with Professor Spencer James of Brigham Young University, Utah – found that most couples who split up had been quite happy with their relationship and not quarrelling too much only a year earlier while they were still together, whether married or not.[13]

One minute they look fine, just like the vast majority of couples who stay together. There is nothing to distinguish them. The next minute they have split up. How on earth did that happen? Remember, this is the case with the majority of family breakdowns.

If it looks pretty odd to us on the outside, might it also have been as big a surprise for the children on the inside? A moment's thought suggests that the split comes out of the blue for the children as well.

As adults, we tend to assume that what's good for us will have a positive knock-on effect for the children. It's not comfortable being around two stroppy adults who are going through a messy divorce. Conflict is not nice for anyone to watch. So, not surprisingly, we want to calm things down, "soothe", as counsellors say, and get the parents to co-operate with one another. Legions of mediators, counsellors, and other assorted professionals thus line up to make divorce "amicable" – resolved privately out of court – rather than "acrimonious" – unpleasant and public. Studies of these approaches generally speak of how mediation or counselling helps the parents to sort things out in a more grown-up way. The benefit to the children from this is usually assumed but rarely investigated.[14]

Yet calming things down and trying to paper over the cracks may not be in children's best interests at all. Children see what's obvious.

- If the parents seem happy, the children are happy.

- If the parents are fighting, the children are unhappy.

- If parents who fight split up, it makes a great deal of sense to the children.

- But if parents who seem happy split up, it makes no sense at all.

The seemingly happy parents solemnly sit their children down – as they did with Judith – and announce that "Mummy and Daddy don't love each other any more". What are the children to think? Has all that they have ever known in their lives just turned out to be a sham? Of course the end of a relationship that seemed to be low in conflict doesn't make sense to the children. It comes out of the blue and it messes with their minds.

***

So, if we're not fighting, and not even especially unhappy, should we stay together "for the sake of the children"?

Let's get back to the Harry and Kate story...

When Kate confronted me in that office, I knew I was in big trouble. But I had absolutely no idea what to do about it.

She said she needed me to be a friend; I thought I was. We were married. We had two lovely young children. We had a good life together. What was it that she wanted?

My biggest fear – the white flash that had shot through my head – was that I was about to lose the children. If ever there was somebody who was desperate to stay together for the sake of the children, I was that person.

I knew I would do whatever it took. But what was that?

***

I was feeling so stuck. I didn't know what to do. I'd said everything to Harry at the meeting, and umpteen times beforehand, but it didn't seem to make any difference. I needed to keep the momentum going. Nothing was changing; I needed some more ideas.

Wise friends of ours, Steve and Ali, had already told me to pull the plug on the one relationship I had that seemed to hold real promise. So I decided to ask them to come and talk to us over dinner, to see if they could come up with any ideas.

During dinner, Ali asked Harry, "What is it you love most about Kate?"

I thought he was going to say, "You're very pretty", "You're attractive", "You're bubbly", or something like that. It would be the sort of lovely thing that a husband might be expected to say about his wife. He'd be proud of me. He'd delight in me.

It took him a while to answer. "I love the way she understands the chemistry of cooking," he said.

I was gobsmacked. I didn't know whether to laugh or cry. His answer was completely and utterly devoid of any emotion or sign of friendship. It sounded ridiculous. If anything, it underlined in bold to Steve and Ali exactly why our marriage was in such trouble.

***

The question completely flummoxed me. "What is it you love most about Kate?"

Believe it or not, I don't think I'd ever really thought about why I loved Kate – or even whether I did. She was just there, the person with whom I was going to share the rest of my life. I liked her; she was great fun and made me feel secure. Did I love her? Yes, in my own way. Did I love anybody? I'm not even sure I knew what love was.

Before the meeting in the vicar's office, I would have struggled just as much if I'd been asked whether I had a happy marriage. I wouldn't have had any idea how to answer that question either. I didn't know what qualities defined happy marriage or even whether ours was happy or not. It just was. After the meeting, it was pretty clear that our marriage was definitely not happy, not from Kate's perspective anyway. As for me, I was still confused.

I tried to put what I love about Kate into words. But the words didn't come. What did I love about her? All I could think was that, as a wonderful cook and now editor of a foodie magazine, Kate could do amazing things with food. She was really impressive. It was like being married to somebody who understands how electricity works. That's what I was thinking. So that's what I said. I couldn't think of anything else at the time.

I didn't see Kate's face as I said it. I saw Ali. She camouflaged the dropping of her jaw long enough to tell me, "Harry, you're so emotionally closed that you're almost psychotic."

I felt rather proud of this. I had no idea what it meant, but it sounded grand.

"I really think you ought to go for counselling," Ali continued. "You need to crack that nut a little bit and see what happens from there."

I had no idea what she was talking about. Even if hesitant to go for counselling – about which I knew nothing, other than that it was a place for Californians to send their poodles – I agreed. The threat of losing the kids was enough to make me do whatever it took.

***

Steve and Ali made me feel very supported. It wasn't just me. They had seen how emotionally closed Harry was. It was a small comfort.

I also began to feel more hopeful. Harry went to counselling once a week for the next few months. I did notice some differences as he began to open up. But, even if this was good for Harry, it still did nothing for our marriage.

We decided that I would come with him for a session. I was feeling particularly low, unsupported, unloved, and lonely in my marriage. I was really fed up. When the counsellor asked me how I was, I burst into tears. She turned to Harry and said, "Come on, Harry, do something." He just sat there motionless, staring at me.

He did nothing.

We didn't talk to each other when we left. Harry had to go back to work and I had to go back home to rescue the kids.

When I got home, I knew I had nothing left to give. I had lost hope. I was stuck. I put the children in front of the TV and sat down to write a letter. It was a job spec of what it was like to be Harry's wife. It was very businesslike. My tone was very flat and matter of fact.

I wrote about the terms and conditions.

On the plus side, my "package" included enough money to live comfortably, a nice place to live, and good holidays. In exchange, I would care for the children, cook meals, and clean the flat.

On the minus side, what I really craved was friendship. But it wasn't part of the deal. Would I ever get it?

"WHO KNOWS? WHO CARES?" I wrote the last few words in capitals.

***

Those words shocked me to the core. "WHO CARES?"

I could almost hear Kate's voice as I read the letter. She was showing me the depth of her despair, her sense of capitulation to a life that might have looked good to outsiders, but was empty inside.

For the very first time, I felt something of her pain. I had done this to Kate. It was my lack of love, my neglect, my failure to nurture or cherish her. These were "feeling" words

I could not have used six months earlier: the counselling had made a difference.

I'd read the letter sitting on our bed, where she'd left it for me. I got up and went into the next room to find her.

I don't know why I did it but I dropped to my knees. I'd never felt such compassion for Kate and such shame about myself.

Somewhere in my head, a switch had flicked. I now knew I needed to make our marriage work, not "for the sake of the children", but for Kate. She deserved it. She was worth it. I'd be a fool not to make it up to her.

"You have no reason to believe me, Kate," I said, looking up at her bemused face. "But I'm going to change. I'm so sorry for what I've done."

***

Harry was right about one thing: I had no reason to believe him. Why would I? I'd just written him a letter full of despair and now I felt blank. Anyway, the kids needed feeding and I was tired and worn out. So I didn't expect any change.

But changes did start to happen.

Up to that moment, little casual chats between us about nothing in particular – the sort of thing friends do – had been rare. Afterwards, we did start to talk. They weren't full-blooded, heart-to-heart discussions. And I was sceptical that Harry's new effort might be just some tactic he'd learned from his counselling. Nonetheless, chats started to happen. Maybe not often. But they did occur.

I was also aware that Harry seemed to take a little more interest in me. Compliments had never been his strong suit. Occasionally, through gritted teeth, I would ask, "Do you like what I'm wearing?"

Now I noticed him make compliments without being prompted. It was nice.

If I'm honest, I seemed to have my radar on more for the mistakes than for the good things that Harry did. I was always aware when Harry did something wrong. We might take two steps forward and one step back. But it was the one step back that lodged in my mind, evidence that things hadn't changed at all.

Except that they had.

Happy wife, happy life

Men and women are different. But not because we come from Mars and Venus. In most respects, men and women are from earth. The key difference is that women have babies and men don't. While roles and opportunities have changed for the better, this aspect of human nature means women will always tend to be more child-oriented than men. Women even select themselves out of top jobs in order to accommodate family life. Research on parenting shows that if the mother is happy, then so are the children and the father. Happy dads don't seem to have the same importance.

Kim and David met while at university. Although they hit it off straight away as friends, it was not until several years later that they were able to convert their friendship into romance, marriage, and children. David had always harboured hopes that they could be more than friends; Kim had been more reluctant. Convinced that she was the one, he waited patiently until at last she realized that she wouldn't find anybody better.

By the time the first of their two children was born, David had established himself in a responsible job with the Department of Health, involved with hospital management. This necessarily included regular travel around the country and meant that David was away a lot. Kim put her involvement with a national charity supporting newly released prisoners on hold in order to concentrate on being a new mother.

Both Kim and David are strong, emotionally intelligent characters. But that's about where the similarities end.

Whereas Kim invariably wanted to work through any differences that came up between them, David saw any kind of heated discussion as unnecessary conflict. He preferred to ride out the storm in the belief that time would sort things out. It meant that they clashed. She would become frustrated when he appeared reluctant to talk things through. He found it difficult that Kim wanted to dissect an issue to what he considered an unnecessary level of detail.

Like many new parents learning together how to make their life work, it took them several years to figure out how to manage their different needs and expectations.

Whenever David returned from trips away, the children would clamber all over him. After playing energetically with them, he would almost forget to focus on Kim. While she was delighted that he was such a wonderful father, she needed his attention one way or another. Without it, she felt marginalized and undervalued.

It seemed to her that he was having his cake and eating it. He had a rewarding and responsible job outside the home and was well looked after inside it. He received attention from all directions. She, on the other hand, was stuck at home or with the children all day. Although she loved looking after the children, she was aware that being a mother gets a poor press. The worst question anyone could ask her was, "What do you do?"

Her need for attention often came out in the form of micro-management. "Do this. Do that." It didn't exactly encourage him to want to hang out with her. He still needed space to relax at home, so he tended to withdraw.

Kim and David aren't in any particular marital difficulty. They are a fairly typical couple going through what is probably the most challenging phase of married life: bringing up young children. It means working out roles and making sacrifices and compromises, while being constantly exhausted.

Their biggest problem, as with any two people, is that they are different. It's how they manage those differences that counts.

Today, Kim and David are just beginning to emerge from the fog of life with small children. David is well aware that Kim has temporarily sacrificed her passion for social work in order to be a mother. His own sacrifice is to be committed to making time for his wife every day, even when exhausted after his own long day at work and even when he doesn't feel like it. It's a decision he's made. The effort is always worth it. He has also learned to let Kim talk things through, however uncomfortable it sometimes makes him feel, and however much it flies in the face of his natural instinct to let things sort themselves out on their own.

What's important to her is important to him. Now that she gets more of the attention she needs, he tends to get more of the space he needs. It's a win–win situation. Happy wife, happy life!

***

Andrew and Rachel are also very different, as well as being two of the nicest people you could meet. Originally from opposite ends of the country, they nearly didn't get together in the first place.

They first met at the wedding of a mutual friend, and hit it off. As the more dynamic and proactive of the two, Rachel decided this was a relationship worth pursuing. However, her efforts to travel hundreds of miles to see him seemed destined to end in failure.

She mistook his relaxed, easy-going nature for indifference and indecision. Returning home disconsolate, she was pleased and surprised to find emails waiting for her.

The relationship continued at arm's length for several months until she once again travelled to him. After circling the subject of marriage in their conversations, she got the feeling during a long walk that he was about to propose. He didn't. In her proactive way, she confronted him. "Did you bottle it?"

"Yes," he replied. He rang two days later to propose.

Far from his being indecisive, everything that Andrew does is deeply considered. As an introvert who processes things internally, he is rarely impulsive and always prefers to think things through before reaching a conclusion. This makes him brilliant with routine but hopeless with change. His own career ambitions are secondary to those of his wife and children. On one level, he is therefore a wonderful husband and father. On another level, however, he takes a position of diminished responsibility in the home.

Rachel couldn't be more different. She is ambitious and proactive, running the household and making the decisions. She drives virtually all that happens in their family, such as where they live and what they do; Andrew tends to go along with whatever she says. But this does not make him in any way a doormat. Nor does Rachel take advantage. Their devotion to one another helps them overcome their differences.

One further fundamental difference between them is in the security they feel about family life. Whereas Andrew's experience of growing up was one of happiness and stability, Rachel's parents had a messy separation, which left her fearful that the same might happen to her. On occasion, Andrew's relaxed manner has led to throwaway comments, spoken without thinking, that trigger a real sense of panic and insecurity in Rachel. He is always quick to apologize.

Although they are not a typical couple in that Rachel so obviously makes the decisions, their marriage is strong because Andrew puts Rachel and their children first in all that he does.

Who could want more? Once again: happy wife, happy life.

***

Men and women are different.

That's what most people think, right? We think, feel, communicate, make decisions, behave, and live life in different ways.

Let's begin with an ever so slightly tongue-in-cheek look at how the stereotypical man and woman organize their thoughts.

Men's brains seem to be divided into compartments, with a different one for each activity. A man can operate in only one compartment at a time. At work, he is thinking about work because his mind is in the work compartment. While there, not only will he not be thinking about home, he actually *can't* think about home. Watching sport on TV, he won't also be worrying about the washing up that sits waiting for him in the sink next door. It's not just in another room; it's in a completely different compartment in his head. On a business trip, he will forget to call his wife because he's actually forgotten he has a wife. Every now and then, something he hears or sees will remind him that he needs to change compartments, stop work, and call his wife. While speaking to her, he may still forget to ask about the children. After all, they are in yet another compartment.

The biggest compartment in a man's head is marked "Nothing". When he's in this compartment, the lights are off and nobody is at home. Therefore, the worst question a woman can ever ask a man is, "What are you thinking?"

A man will typically respond to this by muttering or mumbling. He is playing for time as he desperately tries to move to a compartment that has something in it. Only when he gets there, having sweated and stuttered along the way, does he finally have something to talk about. Then he will tell you all he knows about that compartment.

When he communicates with anyone, there are only two possible subjects: either the compartment he happens to be in, or the compartment the other person is in.

His main interest will be his own compartment. So he will try to keep the conversation focused on that compartment, either by reporting its contents or by bringing the subject under discussion back there. The other person's compartment becomes interesting only when he senses there is something wrong with it. Then he will step into the other person's compartment and offer advice and suggestions on how to sort out the problem and clean the place up. The conversation can move on when both of these acts are complete.

A woman's brain, on the other hand, is more like a room full of spinning plates. Each plate represents an area of concern or responsibility. These can range from the very important, such as concern about her mother's failing health, to the more mundane, such as wondering whether the milk got put back in the fridge.

This can mean a great many plates being spun at any one time. Individual plates demand occasional attention, resulting in what can seem like a random progression of thoughts. It is not. It is simply the brain's way of ensuring that none of the things that need attention get forgotten.

Thoughts swirl around randomly so that a typical conversation can jump between wholly unrelated events. This is not quite the famed multitasking. It's more like an ability to switch instantly from one subject to another and yet another, in rapid succession.

One moment, a woman will be attending to the plate that wonders if her son has enough breakfast this morning. The next, her mind has switched onto another plate that worries whether she will be back in time to take the dog out for a pee. Then on to the thank-you letter her son needs to send to Granny for his birthday present, the milk still outside the fridge, her mum's health again, food tonight, and her husband's doctor's appointment. And all this goes through her mind while she is at work, spinning several other plates.

Some of these plates will be more or less permanent, usually those involving family well-being or regular events such as dinner. Others have a sell-by date by which they need to be completed. Each day begins with a whole row of these, such as the need to call her mother. A good day ends with most of the plates successfully removed. A bad day ends with plates spinning through the night and on into the next day, perhaps because other plates got in the way of her making that call.

When she communicates with anyone, all manner of topics can come out of her head in seemingly random fashion. Chores, relationships, and worries dominate because they need constant attention. Some of these plates will keep spinning until they are removed. "The bin needs emptying" is a request rather than a complaint. "I'm tired" is a spinning plate that cannot be removed. It can, however, be acknowledged and understood. When listening to others, she knows the difference.

The result is that a man can seem deeply frustrating to a woman. She gets cross when he doesn't call her when he goes away. She doesn't understand his compartments. At home, he doesn't stay on top of all the things that worry her. He doesn't understand her spinning plates.

Similarly, a woman can seem deeply confusing to a man. It's obvious to him that he cares for her because of the things he does for her. Yet, instead of getting appreciation for fixing that blockage in the washing machine, he is accused of taking too long. Then she reminds him of the two dozen other jobs that need doing. He doesn't understand that he won't ever be able to remove all of her plates. Nor does he get that each plate, big and small, has the same value.

Let's hear how this stereotype applies in the case of Kim and David, whom we met at the start of the chapter.

***

If Kim needs something to be arranged or a relationship problem resolved, David wants to be told about it once. After that, he will log it in a compartment and deal with it in his own time, perhaps later when he can handle it better. In other words, he wants to be left to get on with it. It's OK for Kim to remind him once or twice. If he's asked, "Darling, just checking if you've had time to ...", then that's fair game.

When David doesn't respond at once, it can sometimes feel like a personal affront to Kim. If it's important to her, surely it should be important to him? So she needs to keep checking on him because, for her, this is a plate that will keep spinning until it's removed. It's on her long mental list of things that need doing. When David finally takes responsibility for sorting it out, she can relax and tick it off the list of bills to be paid or jobs to be done that swirls around her head. But, until he does, the spinning continues and she needs to keep pursuing him. She's pretty tenacious when she needs to be, like a dog with a bone.

To David, these constant reminders begin to look like conflict. He hates arguments, and this looks like one. He knows what he has to do but he doesn't want to be badgered about it. The result is that he closes down mentally and retreats to his "cave". He knows that Kim interprets this withdrawal as "He doesn't care". He doesn't stay there long any more. He knows he needs her plate to stop spinning.

***

Do these analogies ring a bell for you?

Stereotypical ways of talking about men and women became popularized by the famous bestseller *Men are from Mars, Women are from Venus*. Writer John Gray cleverly presented some of the ways men and women differ as being as if we are from different planets.[1]

There's an element of truth to all this. But there's also a problem with putting all men into one box and all women into another. Not all men compartmentalize or deal with their stress by withdrawing to their cave. Not all women spin plates and charge after their husband when fired up by a sense of injustice.

One of the best recent investigations of this comes from US social scientists Bobbi Carothers and Harry Reis. Their study looked at over a hundred different ways in which men and women might differ. Their paper is rather ironically titled "Men and women are from earth", which also gives you a pretty good clue to their conclusion.[2]

Imagine for a moment that men and women are painted a different colour. Suppose that all men are coloured blue and all women are coloured red. Colour would then be what Carothers and Reis call a "taxon". Whenever you see somebody wandering around who is painted blue, you can be reasonably certain that that person is a man. If the person is painted red, you can be similarly confident that you are looking at a woman. So, if all you know about people is that men are blue and women are red, then colour is a "taxonic" difference that enables you to identify men and women. Get the idea?

So what isn't a "taxon"? Although there most certainly are stereotypes in the ways that men and women tend to think differently, there is also a great deal of overlap in attitudes and behaviour.

Attitude to sex is one good example covered in the study. Men tend to think about sex more often than women do and are also more likely to find the idea of sex with a stranger more appealing. Women, on the other hand, are less willing than men to have sex without love.

So, if all you know about somebody is that they think about sex a lot and don't mind having sex without love, you might be able to guess that it's a man. However, you couldn't be at all confident about this. Attitude to sex may fit the stereotype. But it isn't a "taxon". There's just too much overlap between the sexes.

Here are some other examples that show average differences between men and women but where there is also a great deal of overlap.

- With regard to our attitudes to finding a potential marriage partner, as well as having a more relaxed attitude to sex, men tend to place more importance on physical looks, whereas women tend to put more emphasis on future prospects.

- As regards the way we relate to one another, men tend to be more competitive, decisive, persistent, and robust, whereas women tend to be more empathetic, emotional, devoted, gentle, helpful, kind, aware of people's feelings, and oriented towards caring for others.

- When it comes to our attributes, men tend to be more interested in science, whereas women are more likely to fear failure.

All these differences fit within the stereotypes. Yet none of them show us traits that are exclusive to either men or women. We all do a bit of both.

Let's leave Carothers and Reis for a second and go back to how the couple David and Kim sometimes deal with issues between them.

***

Kim's natural reaction to injustice or hurt is to confront and pursue it until the problem is solved. She's upset. She wants to talk it out with David. For her, resolution comes through getting it off her chest until she's happy that he understands what's happened. Sometimes that means talking it through more than once. Invariably, it means an apology of some sort. Understanding, kindness, and apology are what remove this particular spinning plate.

David is pretty good at apologizing; just not immediately. When he's done something to hurt Kim, his natural reaction is to deal with it in his own time and way. Usually he knows what he's done, so what she has to say comes as no great surprise. His way out is either to try to solve her problem or to get to the point where he is able to apologize. That can take time. His time. What he doesn't need is to be pushed into a corner; he doesn't much like confrontation. Kim's pursuit makes him feel under pressure. So he ends up shutting down or walking away. Kim then thinks he doesn't care. It's not what either of them wants or intends.

***

David and Kim have fallen into the classic "demand–withdraw" behaviour that is usually pretty unhelpful to relationships.[3] The stereotype is that women demand and men withdraw. But how true is that generally?

A few years ago, Harry ran a survey of new mothers for his book *Let's Stick Together – The Relationship Book for New Parents*. He asked them about how they and their spouse or partner each dealt with arguments.[4]

Most couples used demand–withdraw when they argue. However, for every two stereotypical couples – where the mother demands and the father withdraws – there's one more couple who do it the other way round and yet another who can go either way.[5]

So, when you read about David running to his cave with Kim in hot pursuit, it's still only a minority who will be able to relate to their experience. Some will say, "Nonsense, it's the other way round." Others will say it happens both ways. And plenty of couples won't relate to it at all.

Their experience may fit the stereotype. But it's hardly black and white.

Are there any areas at all where men and women differ in absolute terms, where our differences can be described as a "taxon" rather than just a tendency?

Back to Carothers and Reis again. They found two areas that distinguish men from women much more clearly:[6]

- **Physical attributes and size** differ greatly between men and women. Among male and female college athletes who participated in the track events of high jump, long jump, or javelin throw, there was virtually no overlap in results. So, if you watched somebody jump above a certain height or distance, or throw a javelin particularly far, you could be very confident that you were watching a male athlete and not a female one. You could be equally confident if all you knew about somebody were their body measurements. A separate study of weight, height, shoulder breadth, arm circumference, and waist-to-hip ratio demonstrated that men are almost always physically bigger and stronger than women. There are obviously exceptions to this. But, if all you know about somebody is their strength or size, you can make a pretty good guess at whether they are male or female. This distinction definitely qualifies as a "taxon".

- **Sex-stereotyped activities** also differ greatly. College students were asked to list activities that they liked doing in their spare time. Out of 129 activities listed, twenty-eight showed a tendency to be stereotypically male or female. However, across thirteen of these, there was almost no overlap at all. Boxing, construction, golf, video games, and porn were all predominantly male activities. Taking a bath, talking on the phone, watching talk shows, and various aspects of cosmetics were predominantly female activities. So, if you wander out to the golf course, you can predict with a high degree of confidence that almost all of the players you see will be men. And, if you walk into a room only to discover that a member of your family is watching a chat show on TV, it's also a fair bet that it'll be a woman. These particular activities also count as "taxons".

This is hilarious! But the conclusion is clear. Men's greater strength and size makes them interested in very different activities from women. As Carothers and Reis conclude in their paper, it is easy to see that men's and women's bodies were built to do different things.

There is, of course, one further difference that distinguishes men and women. Ultimately, it's the most important difference, bringing with it a profound difference in mindset and attitude to life.

Women have babies and men don't.

This is one difference that is absolute. Since no man has ever given birth, there is no overlap whatsoever here. If somebody tells you they are pregnant, you can be 100 per cent certain that it's a woman.

Apart from stating the obvious, why is this so important?

Simple.

Nine months of growing a baby inside her unavoidably changes the way a woman thinks when she becomes a mother. For nine months, she is constantly aware that something, somebody, is moving around within her body, expanding her shape, affecting her moods and needs, making her self-conscious, and altering the way she thinks about herself. For nine months, she has non-stop movement, heat, and discomfort that she cannot ignore.

By the time she gives birth, thoughts about the baby have become completely automatic. "Baby, baby, baby" dominates her thinking, pressing on her mind almost continuously. Although the relentlessness of this will ease over time, she will be unable to stop herself from thinking about her baby at the back of her mind, perhaps even for the rest of her life.

Between the two of us (Harry and Kate), we've run hundreds of Let's Stick Together relationship sessions for new parents, in post-natal clinics, in children's centres, in mums and toddler groups.[7] We've spoken to several thousand new mothers about the way pregnancy makes mums think about "baby, baby, baby" automatically.

Every mum agreed. Not a single one disagreed.

***

To illustrate a few of the ways these differences play out in everyday life, consider the following.

A mother's natural orientation towards her children suggests a qualitatively stronger bond compared to the father. So, when we hear a story about a father abandoning his children, we may tut-tut and disapprove but we're not surprised. It's now become sufficiently commonplace that there are whole communities where this happens. It may even be that men are no longer treated as a legitimate and important part of the family system. Instead of drawing them in, women let men off the hook and push them away.

Yet it's still exceptional to hear of a mother who walks out on her family. Indeed, a mother fleeing from her children remains a taboo that retains the power to shock. It almost always involves a woman in need of serious help.

On the other hand, a man's extra physical strength suggests a natural inclination towards protecting his family. Even in unequal households where women still carry a disproportionate share of the domestic burden, heavy chores around the house are still invariably delegated to the man. Most men and women would regard this as utterly reasonable. Few men complain that this is unfair or unequal, because it's so natural.

Very early in our marriage, we were asleep in our first-floor apartment. Suddenly we were woken by the sound of footsteps charging noisily down our staircase. Harry was out of the bed before Kate even had time to prod him. In the darkness, he walked with trepidation to the top of the stairs, heart pumping, tensing himself for action. He looked down at the culprit, a travel bag that had toppled off balance and bounced downstairs.

In most cases, it's the man who will expect, and be expected, to pluck up the courage and investigate. It's hard to imagine too many husbands leaning across to their wife, nudging her, and whispering nervously, "Go and see who that is!" Of course, it's the man who is the protector.

These natural inclinations remain very strong. A recent study from Oxford University[8] showed that even modern fathers of newborns who had every intention of sharing in the role of parent at home found it hard to put into practice. Just about everybody – except the likely culprit, human nature – got a share of the blame for this. Similarly, a UK government-backed survey of new parents found that just 1 per cent of fathers had applied for the government's new paternity leave scheme.[9] Reasons given were that it was financially unworkable, that fathers didn't know about it, and – somewhat revealingly – that 55 per cent of the mothers refused to share their own maternity leave!

The reality is that once a baby arrives, men and women's natural inclinations kick in.

Women make the nest. Men protect the nest.

***

Let's summarize where we've got to.

There are lots of differences between men and women. Most of these reflect an overlap rather than things that only men or only women can do. Men do some things better than women. Women do other things better than men. But these are not absolutes; they are tendencies or averages.

But there are two important characteristics that distinguish men and women much more clearly:

- Mostly, men are physically stronger than women.

- Only women have babies.

It is these characteristics that give us – as men and women – a natural sense of direction in the way we think about family. We're not talking about how individual families divide up roles; who actually changes the nappies, who does the washing up, who brings in the cash. We're talking about where our natural inclinations lie as men and women.

Having said that, these fundamental biological differences make sense of why women throughout history and cultures have directed their main energies towards children and home while men have directed theirs towards protecting and providing for the family.

In the past, these cultural roles matched our natural inclinations. Some argue that this was repressive for women. It undoubtedly was for some, forced by tradition to stay at home and inhibit their desire to be creative or constructive outside the home. But, by and large, this was a family system that went with the grain of human nature. Men and women both played to their natural inclination.

Today, equal opportunity has given women full access to the workplace. It's a tremendous piece of social progress. A survey of American mothers by Pew Research found that most of them want to work. Half would prefer that work to be part-time.[10]

British studies suggest much the same thing. A big study by Professors Alison Booth and Jan van Ours looked at British parents and childless couples over a seven-year period.[11] Of the mothers, they found that about one-third had part-time jobs – less than thirty hours per week – and another third worked full-time. Mothers tended to be happiest with their job if they worked part-time and happiest with their life either if they worked at all or when their children started going to school.

Among fathers, almost none worked part-time. Fathers tended to be happiest merely if they had a job.

What this shows is that both mothers and fathers want to work. But mothers differ from fathers in that they tend not to find the work especially satisfying unless it's part-time.

In spite of this, a lot more mothers than fathers still say their status as a working parent makes it harder both to get on in the workplace and to be a good parent.[12] And although there are signs of change, fathers are still not rushing to take on extra housework.[13] Nor are these gender roles changing nearly as much as policy-makers might hope or expect.

An awful lot has happened in recent years in respect of social attitudes and family policy. There's been a boom in childcare, not least through the introduction of Sure Start children's centres throughout the UK as well as various tax allowances that help parents subsidize the cost of childcare. There's also been a big push towards paternity leave that encourages parents to exchange work and family roles as equals, rather than assume that mum stays home and dad goes to work.

We wanted to find out how these roles had changed over time, especially in families where one parent works and one stays at home. So we commissioned some data from the Office for National Statistics especially for this book, going back fifteen years.[14]

It was hard to know what to expect. Everything we saw and heard in the media suggested that the stereotypical one-earner family was on the way out. Everything we knew about human nature suggested that mums still wanted to care for their young children themselves. The net result was that we expected to find fewer one-earner families as economic pressures pushed more mums out to work. We also thought more dads would be staying at home, freeing up mum to go out to work.

We were wrong on both counts.

Despite all these social changes, and despite all the political encouragement to parents to get out and work, there has been virtually no change in the proportion of one-earner families. Nor has there been any noticeable shift from mums staying at home to dads staying at home.

Fifteen years ago, nine out of ten parents at home with children up to the age of eleven were mothers. The same is true today.

In other words, new social policies and huge pressure on parents to change the way they mix work and childcare have had little to no effect on whether they stay at home rather than go to work – and almost no effect on the traditional one-earner model where the mother stays at home and the father works.

Women have more opportunity than ever to get out of the home and into work. Yet they are not taking it. For the time being at least, human nature tops social incentives.

***

Our oldest daughter has just qualified as a doctor. As parents, we are unbelievably proud of what she has achieved. And, of course, it's extremely useful to have a doctor in the family – just as it would be to have a plumber or an electrician or a rich investment banker!

As part of her final year at medical school, she was sent for one of her rotations to a hospital that happens to be near where we live. Once a week, she would bring a group of hungry young medics over to our house for food, sustenance, and a break from the rigours of their training.

Over the weeks of their placement, we got to know several of these stars of the future well. But one of the first questions we asked each of them when we met was about their career plans. The gender divide in answers was striking. While a study of just a handful of people is not very scientific, our discussions were highly illuminating.

Without exception, each of the young women said they had started out at medical school five years earlier with the highest of expectations. Although they all knew that some two-thirds of doctors on their course would end up as general practitioners, none of them planned to go down that route. They were all going to end up as surgeons or gynaecologists or some other highly demanding and specialized job.

And yet, five years on, every one of them now admitted that they had toned down their initial expectations. Each of them told us how they still thought these specializations were wonderful. But over time they had come to realize that such highly demanding roles were "just not compatible with the kind of family life I want to lead". All were now thinking of completing their two foundation years as newly qualified doctors and then heading into general practice, still rewarding and challenging work, but a role in which they could work more flexibly.

In other words, even before any of them had children of their own, the prospect of motherhood was looming ever larger on their radar. All of them were already thinking about how to balance work and family life.

As for the single male medic who came to dinner with them, he was unhesitating in his response. "Plastic surgeon," he replied.

All of these young professionals have the capacity and intelligence to take on more or less any job within the medical world. And yet some women – it may even be "many women", although it's obviously not "all women" – are selecting themselves out of the more demanding roles in anticipation of becoming mothers.

Human nature is hard to buck.

***

It would seem that the cultural desire for mums to work is clashing with women's natural inclination to prioritize home life, and losing. But the point of this book is not to tell mums whether they should work or stay at home. You must do whatever is right for you.

What really matters is whether mums are happy. And this has a much greater influence on family life than whether dads are happy. Here's what the latest research is finding:

- Happy wives tend to have happy husbands, but not vice versa.[15]

- Happy mums tend to produce happy kids.[16]

- Happy marriage tends to lead to happy life and less depression.[17] (This applies to both wives and husbands).

- Happy mums tend to have a stronger effect than happy dads on the well-being of their teenage children.[18]

- Happy wives influence the values of their husbands, but not vice versa.[19]

- Happier wife leads to happier life.[20]

Overall, what these studies are saying is that the extent to which both men and women enjoy their life depends a great deal on having a happy marriage. But a happy wife has a lot more impact on her immediate family than a happy husband.

There's more detail about these findings in the Notes at the end of the book.

***

In an age of equality and equal opportunity, it might seem odd that the happiness of the mother appears more important to family life than the happiness of the father. But, to us, this distinction boils down to human nature and these two key differences between men and women.

The unique characteristic of being a mother – her "taxon" – is her experience of pregnancy. Those nine months automatically condition women's brains to orient themselves more naturally towards their children and the home environment. If they are happy with this set-up, then all is likely to be well in their wider family life.

There's bound to be some overlap with men's happiness here. It's intuitively obvious that, in most cases, if one spouse is happy, so will the other be. But the research points in one direction.

Mum's happiness has a bigger effect on those around her.

The unique characteristic of being a father – his "taxon" – is his extra strength and size. This is bound to orient him towards areas of life where he can use this to his family's best advantage. This in no way excludes him from looking after the children. But his natural inclination is going to be towards protecting and providing for his family. How he achieves this might matter a great deal to him. But it's much less important to the success of his marriage and the well-being of his children.

Fundamentally, what matters most in the family is mum. She is the centrepiece around which the rest of the family rotate, regardless of whether she works or stays at home.

Until now, public policy has focused mostly on who does what in respect of roles. Creating more opportunities for mum to work and dad to look after the children is good, but it won't strengthen families. We need to start thinking about family in a different way, by recognizing mum's role at the centre of family life and working out what mums want.

The secret of successful family life is this: a happy mum makes a happy family.

What mums want

Everyone wants reliable love. But in a world with family breakdown at record levels, how do we find it? Before having children, men and women are quite similar. Having a child changes everything. Through surveys and interviews, we show how the number-one thing mums want from dads is friendship. The solution to building stronger families is radical and countercultural, yet utterly compelling. Husbands, love your wives. And they will love you right back.

Everyone wants reliable love.

Babies thrive with a mother's love. Children and teenagers thrive in a secure home where they know they are loved. Adults thrive in the love of another.

All through our lives, we operate best when we know that we are loved. Not just loved today. Not just loved because we are behaving well. We need to know that we will be loved tomorrow and into the future, no matter what.

Humans are not designed to live life alone. When we are babies, our parents meet that need. As children and teens, we begin to venture out from the home and add friendships. As adults, most of us form a new home and attach ourselves to another adult.

When two of us get together to form a relationship, we create a new identity as a couple. As well as a "me" and a "you", there is now an "us".[1]

As our relationship grows, our new identity as a couple becomes more and more important. Each of us will then make it a priority to spend time together. We will give up other options in order to do that, including taking ourselves off the market. We are now an item, and it feels good. With our best feet forward, we will disregard or overlook things that clash with this new ideal. Willingness to forgive and sacrifice for one another comes easily. We start to talk about ourselves in terms of "we" and "us" and we begin to sense the possibility of a future together.

DEDICATION

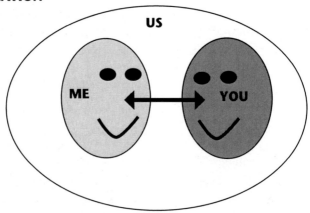

When we think of commitment, we are thinking of the extent to which we see ourselves as a couple with a future. Researchers call this internal bond "dedication" or "interpersonal commitment".[2] There is also another type of external commitment that constrains couples and makes it harder to leave. Constraints – such as having children or living together – mean that when the going gets tough, our tendency is to stick at it, even if things are less wonderful than we'd hoped.

The ultimate step of dedication is getting married. We are deliberately buying into a lifetime together as a couple. Where there was lingering doubt or anxiety or ambiguity, such a step brings clarity and intent and the prospect of a love that will last for life.

At least that's the plan. Everyone knows that not all marriages work out. Across the English-speaking world, divorce rates hover at around 40 per cent.[3] That's pretty high. The other way of looking at this is that 60 per cent of marriages – the majority – do work out.

But something important seems to happen when we pop that question, "Will you marry me", and receive the answer, "Yes". Both of us buy into a joint plan for the future, which makes us just as likely to enjoy the fun times but more likely to stick it out through the difficult times.

Would we, Kate and Harry, have split up if we had not been married? Who knows. But our underlying dedication to one another, our intended plan for a life together, meant that we weren't about to give up too easily.

While it's undoubtedly true that couples can be equally dedicated to one another without getting married, the evidence shows it's a whole lot less likely.

Harry's research for Marriage Foundation looked at one of the biggest household surveys in the UK, called Understanding Society.[4]

In families with teenage children, just two out of ten mothers who were married when their child was born had subsequently split up. In sharp contrast, seven out of ten mothers who had never married had subsequently split up. Somewhat surprisingly, six out of ten mothers who married after their child was born subsequently split up. Mother's age and education made no difference to these odds.

So whether couples stay together while they are bringing up their children depends more than anything else on whether they were married beforehand.

If you're reading this and you're not married, it is by no means the end of the world. The odds may not be in your favour, but you can change the odds so that they are. After all, marriage is all about commitment. Dedication is what matters if you want reliable love. You can achieve that without getting married – after all, three out of ten couples manage this perfectly well – but both of you need to be really clear about your decision to be a couple with a permanent future.

You can make this decision as a private agreement between the two of you. But it's a whole lot more obvious and unambiguous if you do it in front of friends and family. A couple of US studies have shown a link between the number of guests at a wedding and couples' subsequent happiness that's nothing to do with how much you spend.[5] The theory is that because you're taking such a risk by marrying one person and giving up all your other options, you feel a whole lot more confident about that choice if there's a load of people patting you on the back and saying well done!

Regardless of whether you marry or not, if you want to stay together, both of you need to be really clear about your plan to stay together for life. Both of you need to have bought into the project, having made your own individual decision and not been pressured into it.

Another of Harry's studies shows how divorce rates in the early years of marriage are plummeting. In the UK, divorces are granted to one spouse or the other depending on who does the filing. It turns out that almost all of this recent fall reflects fewer divorces being granted to wives. Divorces granted to husbands have barely changed. What's almost certainly happened is that in recent years, with less and less pressure to marry, those men who do marry have really bought into it.[6]

In the words of Professor Scott Stanley, a leading researcher in how commitment works, they "decide" rather than "slide". Fewer "sliders" and more "deciders" means more committed men and therefore fewer disgruntled wives filing for divorce.[7]

So, if you want to stay together, if you want reliable love, if you want friendship, dedication is all you need.

***

Peter and Elena came to see us a few years ago. They were married and had two young children. Their marriage was going through difficulties – they didn't specify what when they phoned – but they said they needed help.

When they arrived, we began with our usual introduction. We told them what they could expect from us, how we wouldn't take sides, how our priority was their marriage and how to make it work better than before, in so far as that was both possible and fruitful. We told them we would begin by hearing their story from each of their perspectives, observe how they interacted together, point out what we thought needed to change to get them back on track, and help them come up with a route map for the immediate future. Our first session would focus on hearing their story and sharing a little of our own, as a symbol of hope that they are not alone and that there are ways through these things.

Elena started. She and Peter had met through a church group. Peter worked in the growing field of computers and IT, and Elena was an administrator at a primary school. They quickly fell in love and spent every opportunity outside work together. Elena had always dreamed of being married and living a life built around family. Peter fitted the bill perfectly. He was trustworthy, he worked hard, and – most of all – he made her feel special. It seemed only natural to Elena that their relationship would lead to marriage.

After a year together, the subject of marriage was firmly on Elena's mind. Increasingly, it slipped out into their conversations so that it was no great surprise when Peter proposed. They married in church six months later and began to build a life together. The arrival of their two children made Elena's life complete at home. The icing on the cake was that she could supplement Peter's income by working part-time at the school, which was happy to have her on any terms at all.

Then the bomb dropped. Ten years into their marriage and with their two children now safely established at primary school, Elena found out that Peter was having an affair. That was two weeks ago.

At this point in the story, unsurprisingly, Elena burst into tears. She was clearly devastated. The news was still raw. Peter looked emotionless. But he did lean towards her, reach out his hand, and gently hold her arm. It was a good sign.

After a suitable pause, we asked Peter to tell his version of the story.

Factually, Peter concurred with Elena's timeline of events. But that was about as far as the similarities went. Yes, he had fallen in love with her and enjoyed her company enormously. But, even early in their first year together, he had begun to sense a growing inevitability to their relationship, with which he wasn't entirely comfortable.

Elena's frequent mentioning of marriage made her intentions and expectations clear. Most of the time he could palm it off with laughter, as if he too felt the same way. It wasn't that he didn't love her; he did. He just wasn't quite as convinced as she was that their entire lives and future together should be so clearly defined. Eventually, her persistence paid off and he proposed.

As he told this story to Elena, her eyes were misting up, her face filled with love and confusion. It was obvious that she was hearing about his doubts for the first time.

Peter said that getting married was like getting onto a train into which he was then locked. He couldn't get off. After the wedding, he told her, he had spent the first six months of their marriage in turmoil.

Elena's mouth dropped open in astonishment. She had had no idea. She looked at us and around the room in bewilderment, barely listening as he finished his story, of the arrival of children, of his feeling of being neglected, of the drinks after work with an understanding female work colleague, of the one thing that led to another.

It was a classic case of "sliding" rather than "deciding". Peter had never really bought in. There was little or no point trying to teach them practical communication skills, how to resolve conflict, how to avoid the little bad habits that destroy relationships, or anything else that could normally hope to improve and strengthen a relationship.

In the end, it was all about commitment. Her dedication to him remained total. Even after all he had done to betray her and their children, she was still willing to work through his aberration and try to make their marriage work. She was devoted to him and the prospect of their life together as a family.

His dedication to her, on the other hand, was shaky. All that was keeping him in the marriage were the external constraints that made it hard for him to leave, mainly his children but also the embarrassment of facing friends and family. After all, he was the guilty party who had cheated on his wife. With his lover waiting in the wings, Peter was no longer even bound to his own home.

The only possible way ahead was for him to do what he should have done in the first place. He needed to decide to be kind to his wife and put her at the top of his list of priorities, to buy into that vision of living life together, of growing old together, as a married couple. Only when he had made that decision for himself could he hope to enjoy what he already had, a loving and lovely wife and two children who needed him.

Alas, we can't tell you whether this story has a happy ending or not. Peter and Elena thanked us for our time and left. We have never seen them again.

The awful thing is that if anyone had sat Peter down ten years earlier and asked him if he was sure he wanted to get married, this whole crisis could have been avoided.

Maybe he would have realized he couldn't go through with it and walked away. We've known people who have cancelled quite late in the day. It would have been unbelievably distressing for Elena, but, without children, the consequences would have been a lot less serious and each of them would have had the opportunity to find somebody new and better suited for a life together.

Maybe he would have realized that, having been confronted early enough, he could buy into the prospect of a life together after all. Having done so, many of his fears might have ebbed away and he would have found it a great deal easier to put Elena first in his life and resist any fleeting temptations at work.

What Elena needed, more than anything, was a man who was committed to her. She wanted reliable love. It's not too much to ask, is it?

***

As well as reliable love and commitment, what else do mums want? What better way to find out than to ask mums themselves!

Especially for this book, we set up an online survey. Considering the relatively small scale of our mailing list and social networks, the response was pretty remarkable. Within days we had 291 responses.[8]

Mums were clearly eager to have their say.

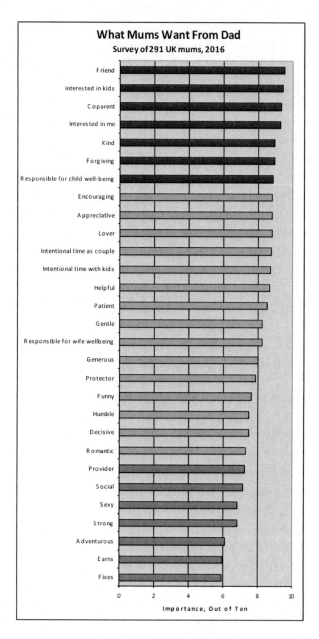

What Mums Want From Dad

Survey of 291 UK mums, 2016

Importance, Out of Ten

We started by asking mums to rate the importance of thirty different qualities or roles or characteristics they might consider important in a husband or partner. The range of scores tells us a lot about what really matters.

At the top of the list was a husband who is a "Friend". Nobody at all rated this below "Moderately Important", equivalent to seven out of ten. Nearly three-quarters rated it as "Extremely important", equivalent to ten out of ten.

At the bottom of the list was a husband who "Fixes things" or "Earns a decent salary". Half of the women in our survey rated "Earns a decent salary" as "Neutral" or lower in terms of importance. Only four mums in our entire survey rated it as "Extremely important", equivalent to ten out of ten.

On its own, this tells quite a story and is worth stating again.

- Most mums say having a husband who is a friend is extremely important: ten out of ten.

- In sharp contrast, only a handful of mums say having a husband who earns a decent salary is extremely important.

So a husband who sees his prime role as earner or man about the house is very much on the wrong track. On average, mums rate these provider/fixer roles as only slightly more important than "Neutral".

On the other hand, a husband who puts friendship at the top of the list is definitely pointing in the right direction. Friendship is "Extremely important" to the vast majority of women.

After friendship, the other qualities that mums said really mattered were being interested in the children, being a co-parent, being interested in mum, being kind, and being forgiving.

After that came taking responsibility for the children's well-being, being encouraging, being appreciative, being a lover, being purposeful about doing things as a couple, and being purposeful about doing things with the children.

At the bottom end of the scale, the qualities that mums said mattered less – after fixing things and earning a decent salary – were being an adventurer, strong, sexy, sociable, and a provider.

Some pretty strong themes jump out from these responses:

- What mums rate as most important is a man who focuses inwards on his family, who prioritizes his relationship with his wife and treats her as a friend with kindness, and also prioritizes his relationship with his children.

- What mums rate as less important are all the things that focus a man outwards from his family: the way he provides, fixes things, uses his strength, goes on adventures, looks great, and socializes well.

- When we looked separately at what happy and unhappy mums wanted, there was a remarkable level of agreement. Happy or not, mums tend to want the same things.

So that's what mums want in respect of qualities, what they want dad to be like.

Let's now have a look at what mums want with regard to priorities, what they want dad to put first

We gave mums a list of ten priorities and asked them how important each of these was to them, how important each was to their husband, and how important they think each should be to their husband!

The ten priorities were "dad", "mum", "dad's time and space", "mum's time and space", "dad's work", "mum's work", "home admin" (tax/money/bills), "home chores" (clean/tidy/shop/cook), "maintenance" (fixing), and "the children".

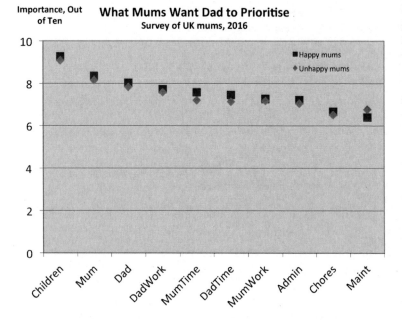

Importance, Out of Ten

What Mums Want Dad to Prioritise
Survey of UK mums, 2016

■ Happy mums
◆ Unhappy mums

X-axis: Children, Mum, Dad, DadWork, MumTime, DadTime, MumWork, Admin, Chores, Maint

The clear answer from mums was that they want dads to prioritize "the children" most of all, followed by "mum", and then "dad" and "dad's work".

All the boring stuff – "maintenance", "chores", and "admin" – comes way down the list.

Three things jump out from this:

- First, this affirms what we've just learned – that mums want dads to be focused inwards on the needs of their family.

- Second, once again there's almost no difference between what happy and unhappy mums want from dad. What mums want seems to be remarkably consistent.

- Third, mums want dad to put himself and his work way up the list of priorities. Even if the children and mum come right at the top of the list, mums don't want this to be at the expense of making himself a low priority. They want dad to have a life too.

Now that we know what mums want – for dad to be a friend, interested in them and their children, and to be kind – what do mums and dads actually prioritize in real life?

It'll be no surprise to hear that pretty well all mums – happy and unhappy – put children at the top of their own list of priorities. After that comes dad, and then chores. Also not surprisingly, dad comes before chores when mum is happy and below chores when she is not!

At last we've found a difference between what happy and unhappy mums prioritize. Happy mums attach a greater importance to both dad and themselves, and to each of their work and each of their time, than unhappy mums do. Where mums don't differ is in the importance they attach to children and all the domestic stuff.

Now it's not clear from this whether mums put a higher priority on dads and themselves because they are happy or whether mums become happy as a result. Maybe it doesn't matter.

What does matter is that mums, happy or not, put children and each other at the top of their list of priorities and think husbands should do the same. Work remains important. Most of the boring domestic stuff is way down the list.

But there are two big differences between mums' and dads' priorities. The first is that mums – happy or not – put "chores" near the top of their own list of priorities and near the bottom for their husband. The second is that mums put themselves way down the list whereas they think their husband should put himself near the top.

Hmmm!

Now comes the crunch. As regards what husbands actually prioritize – rather than what their wives think they should prioritize

– there's another big difference between the happy mums and the unhappy ones.

Happy mums differ from unhappy mums in the importance attached by dads to children, to mum, and to home life. However, mums seem to be quite happy when dads put a high degree of importance on work and a relatively low degree of importance on domestic chores.

So the crucial issue is not what dads think about work and chores; it's where the children and mum come in the pecking order that counts.

Mums still value their husband's work and want it to be high on the list of his priorities. They just don't want it to dominate quite as much. Children and wife should come first and work second.

Mums do want a bit more of a helping hand with the chores. That doesn't mean husbands should prioritize chores as much as wives do. Wives – happy or not – still put chores high up on their own list of priorities and low on the list for their husband.

What mums want is a husband who shows he is thinking about his wife and children, and not just about himself and his work.

They don't want husbands to be doormats. They want them to value their work, themselves, and their own time. But mums also need to know they are top of the pecking order and not somewhere down the list as an afterthought.

***

In the last chapter we noted that the biggest difference between men and women is that women have babies and men don't. So a woman's desire for a husband with an inward wife-oriented and child-oriented focus corresponds exactly to what you'd expect.

But let's go back to life before children, where this difference hasn't yet come into play.

With the exception of our personal health and well-being, pretty well all that happens to us in life – for men and women alike – takes place outside our body. Most of what we do and think revolves around the way we engage with the world outside ourselves.

Men and women are primarily outward-looking creatures, both in search of identity, reliable love, and a sense of mission. All of us want to know who we are, where we came from, and where we're going: present, past, and future. Therefore, before we have children, men and women alike are looking for relationship and some sort of meaning and purpose to our lives. We fill our time accordingly with work and play.

A series of fascinating studies by Elianne van Steenbergen and colleagues at Utrecht University in the Netherlands show that when couples work long hours, both spouses tend to become happier.[9] Clearly, not all couples thrive on long hours. But, for most, the long hours and fulfilling work tend to spill over into their enjoyment of life at home. Without other competing roles for either of them, the couple have the capacity and resources, in terms of time and money, to enjoy their work outside the home and their relationship within the home. For both of them, long hours at work represent an investment in their joint future.

This positive connection between work and play is especially strong when it comes to husband's work hours and wife's relationship satisfaction. In other words, both husbands and wives – but especially wives – appreciate their spouse's efforts to bring home the bacon.

She interprets his hard work as a sign that he is committed to their future together. It's reliable love. It's dedication. It's all good!

Everything changes when they have a child.

Whereas before they become parents the husband's long hours at work are viewed in a positive light, after they become parents his long hours at work begin to look like an attempt to get away from home and family. Her maternal focus has shifted to the home. What happens within the home now matters more to her than what happens to protect or provide for their future. His long hours at work begin to make it look as if he doesn't care. She then starts to view their relationship less positively. Worst of all is if the husband actually enjoys his work. It merely rubs salt into the wound.

***

Let's have a look at how this works, in diagram form.

Actually, because this process mirrors our own personal experience so strongly, let's call the happy couple Harry and Kate!

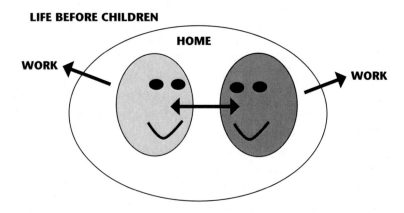

LIFE BEFORE CHILDREN

HOME

WORK

WORK

Kate and Harry start off with a nice balance between home and work life. As their relationship develops, they enjoy thinking about their new identity as a couple. With only work to distract them, it's fairly easy to make time for one another as a couple and have a lot of fun together. Both of them work hard. Work life is a big positive, affirming their plans for their joint future. All in all, their sense of dedication towards one another is strong. In their case, it's a natural progression to formalize their plans for a life together by getting married.

A couple of years on and Kate becomes pregnant with their first child. The arrival of a baby changes everything. Kate temporarily gives up her work in order to focus on life as a new mother. Her nine months of pregnancy have made her highly attuned to the needs of the baby. Harry is equally thrilled with his new role as a father but also knows he is now carrying the weight of the family's financial well-being on his shoulders. He has become the sole provider.

Initially, the excitement and unfamiliarity of new parenthood works in their favour as a family unit. Their relationship remains strong and their identity as a couple is strengthened by the new sense of mission as parents together.

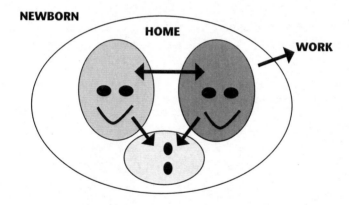

All good so far...

Kate utterly loves being a mother. But, pretty soon, her automatic focus on the new baby and home life begins to chip away at her ability to give attention to Harry. Meanwhile, Harry continues to love being a father but defers to Kate's greater emotional investment as the primary parent. Because she is the one who is constantly thinking about the baby, Kate also makes most of the decisions, whether that's anything to do with the home set-up, the baby's sleeping and feeding routines, how to respond to cries in the night, what clothes and types of nappy the baby should wear, what creams and oils work best, and eventually what sort of food to give the baby.

Because she thinks about these things all the time, Kate states her conclusions with great conviction. Harry tends to go along with what she wants. This doesn't stop Harry continuing to be involved as a father. But, in the same way that Kate takes her eye off the ball regarding their relationship in order to focus on the baby, Harry keeps his mind focused on his responsibility to work hard, which means he reluctantly lets go of any previous ideas he may have had about being a 50:50 parent. Similarly, seeing Kate's focus on the baby, he stops prioritizing time and fun with Kate.

Almost imperceptibly, they begin to drift apart as a couple. Without even realizing it, their priorities have shifted, reflecting the most obvious natural differences between men and women.

DRIFTING APART

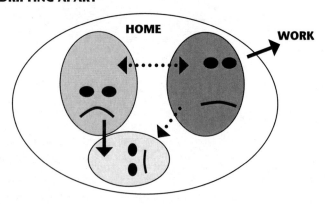

Before having children, each of them could juggle the two priorities of work and marriage almost effortlessly. Even though Kate has temporarily given up work, her world is now consumed by thoughts of the new baby. It's not surprising that she now puts less effort into making time for Harry.

Harry, on the other hand, has more choice in the matter. He doesn't have that constant preoccupation with the baby rolling through his head twenty-four hours a day. When Kate puts her baby down and walks out of the room, her mind is still in the room. When Harry walks out of the room, his mind is moving on to the next subject.

But Harry does still love his wife and want the best for her. But, instead of maintaining the priority of his marriage, and making sure that Kate's well-being remains uppermost while she focuses on the baby, he has allowed Kate to take prime responsibility for home life, turned his attention outwards, and focused on work.

Whereas initially Kate was distracted by the arrival of their new baby, she now notices that Harry no longer gives her the attention he did previously. She doesn't realize that her natural and automatic inward focus on the baby has subtly pushed him away towards his own natural and automatic outward focus on protecting the family.

If only Harry knew what Kate needed. She hints at it again and again. "I just need you to be my friend," she says. "I am," he replies. He is working hard for the family and helping with the baby. Why can't she see that? But she doesn't see it and he never really gets it.

With their marriage no longer being actively fed, and their eyes no longer on each other, Harry and Kate drift apart.

Because so much of his time is spent outside the home, Harry is less aware of the shortcomings in his deteriorating marriage. He finds his purpose and satisfaction in his work. At home, however, he feels that he is constantly on the back foot. Praise for his successes is hard to come by. Mistakes are there to be spotted. But as long as he contributes by doing chores and doing his bit with the baby, he can keep criticism at bay. He is well aware that he and Kate no longer have time for fun together any more. He barely notices that they rarely talk about anything other than work and baby.

Because so much of her time is spent at home, Kate is acutely aware of the shortcomings in her deteriorating marriage. She finds her purpose and satisfaction in life in being a mother. Yet, much as she loves the role, she misses the challenge and stimulation of work. It would be all right if she felt valued by Harry. But, at the end of each day, the constant attention required by caring for a small, vulnerable, dependent, and not always rational child takes its toll. When Harry gets back from work, all she wants is for him to take over so that she can have some time for herself. Yet, even when he does, she can't quite let go of the responsibility for what needs doing next, all those spinning plates that continue to need attention. She assumes Harry will get things right, which he does mostly. But, whenever he does something that she wouldn't do, she is quick to notice.

In Harry and Kate's real-life situation, the arrival of a second child causes their deteriorating marriage to descend into crisis. Their respective roles as homemaker and provider become entrenched. Without thinking about it, it is assumed that Kate will do more of the parenting as Harry goes out and earns the money. Even if both play their part very well, their relationship becomes purely functional.

Eventually Kate confronts Harry with the fact that all is not well in their marriage. This realization comes out of the blue to him.

So what is it that mums want?

WHAT MUMS WANT

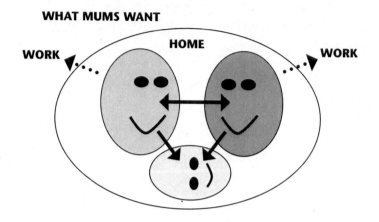

The message from our survey is clear.

What a mum wants is a friend. She wants a husband whose first priority lies within the home, with his children and his wife. Everything revolves around that inward focus on the family.

By making his wife his number-one priority, he will unavoidably want to do whatever he can to bless her, to be involved in her world, to be a thoughtful co-parent who takes responsibility for his children's well-being, and to work hard to support his family.

As her friend, he will be interested in her, treating her with kindness and encouraging her as a person in her own right, in her roles as wife and mother, and in her own work. He will love her and show appreciation of what she does and who she is. And he will be deliberate about his time with her as a couple every bit as much as he is purposeful about his time with the children.

What she is not asking him to do is take over her domestic world and become a doormat or slave. She wants him to maintain his focus on work and also to make time for himself. She is happy taking the lion's share of the chores, but wants him to show willing.

What a mum wants is a husband who, above all else, loves his wife. When he does that, and only when he does that, will she be able to lift her attention from home and children and focus back on him.

So this is what mums want:

Husband, love your wife. Then she will love you right back. In that order.

Learning to love

For many important things in life, there's no manual. The skills of family life and parenthood tend to be passed on automatically. But, as extended families decline, success as a family unit depends more on the community around you. The good news is that you can learn how to have a great marriage. Courses are based on the skills most commonly found among successful couples. Harry and Kate tell the story of the marriage weekend where they fell in love after nine years of marriage.

Hang out for long enough with any group of couples or parents and sooner or later you'll hear somebody say, "Marriage doesn't come with a manual" or "Kids don't come with a manual".

What they really mean is that making life work as a couple or parent can be hard. The easy bit was winning your spouse's heart in the first place. The hunt for a mate, with all its excitement and anxiety, is over. The commitment of getting married has removed any lingering ambiguity about your relationship. You are both on the same page.

But maintaining fun, friendship, love, and laughter in everyday life can be a strange mixture of humdrum and pressurized. The home still needs to be cleaned. Life still has to be managed. Bills still need to be paid. Work is still uncertain. Employers are "committed" until they change their mind. And then come children to complicate things further.

So it's hardly surprising that relationships are difficult. People don't behave the way we'd like. *We* don't behave the way we'd like. It's easy to feel isolated, cut off, abandoned, alone, unsupported, misunderstood, or disappointed. It's easy to sink into despair or hopelessness. We get bored or stuck in a rut. We take each other for granted.

At that point everyone in the group nods and sympathizes. They've felt it too. It's tough.

But there are manuals. If you're lucky, *you* are the manual. It was built into you by your parents. You are the legacy of a strong and stable family who brought you up with great wisdom and love. Now it's your turn to live it out for yourself.

This is the single biggest argument for why strong, stable families matter. They are far more likely to produce a confident and fruitful next generation, who can then repeat the process.

For the rest of us, there are manuals in the shops: the bookshelves are groaning with books on marriage and parenting. And there are also wonderful courses that can be surprisingly helpful and are not at all embarrassing.

The skills that make a great marriage can be learned.

From the night that Harry read my "job-spec" letter, things had definitely got better. But they got better in a two-steps-forward, one-step-back sort of way.

I really appreciated the compliments Harry now gave me. He regularly noticed the way I looked and would then say something nice about me. He hadn't done that before.

But we still didn't have the truly intimate relationship that I craved. I wanted him to be my best friend, to feel relaxed in my company, to be able to spend time chatting with me in the evening, talking about things that friends talk about.

Instead, he would definitely be interested in my day when he got back from work. And I felt much more supported as a mother in what I did at home with the children. But we still rarely talked much about him or me or us. There was a lot of room for improvement in the quality of our conversations. Progress was real but frustrating.

Friends had been telling me of a marriage course that they recommended. By good fortune, there was one coming up near where we lived. I got really excited about it. Even Harry thought it was a good idea, and I felt encouraged that he cared enough. A lot of men would be dismissive about the whole idea, or say they didn't need it because their marriage was fine, or come up with some other excuse.

The fact that the course was full and we'd have to wait until the next year actually made us even more keen to go. So when the phone rang and we were offered a course in a neighbouring country two days later (we were still living overseas), we jumped at it.

***

As I had already got out of my comfort zone by going for a few sessions with a counsellor, the idea of going on a marriage course didn't seem as off-putting to me as it might have done previously. Being turned away because the course was full merely increased my determination to go. So, when the phone rang with a last-minute offer, I said yes before I'd even checked with Kate.

Kate and I needed to do something different to move our marriage up a gear. I had no idea what that something might be. I hadn't had any idea how counselling could help, yet it had: I'd learned about myself. So why not learn how to have a great marriage?

This particular course – called "Marriage Encounter" – ran in a series of cycles. Two couples would give a talk, then we would individually write some thoughts in a private letter to our spouse, and finally, after reading each other's letter, we would have a chat on our own.

I loved the way the course taught me a vocabulary of feelings, how I could feel happy, sad, excited, disappointed, etc. It also taught me how to elaborate more on what these feelings looked like, how I could feel "trapped like a bird in a cage" or "trapped like a rat in a corner". These word pictures conveyed life in a way that was more vivid than I'd ever experienced before.

I found I could say things to Kate in a letter that I might never have been able to say verbally. As I had been so emotionally closed for years, writing it all out gave me a freedom to be romantic, expressive, and emotional, and to dig deep. Feelings are neither right nor wrong. They just are. So I knew that whatever I said couldn't be disputed.

More importantly, reading Kate's letter gave me an insight into what it was like to be her. Because I had previously been so unaware of anything I might have felt, it had never occurred to me to listen to the underlying feelings in what somebody else was saying.

I felt free, like a bird!

***

Well, well. Almost as soon as we arrived, I realized that the tables had turned. I didn't care for the idea of writing about my feelings.

It was my turn to be reluctant and sceptical. Instead, Harry was the one who was enthusiastic about making our marriage work.

Then the most extraordinary thing happened. At first, neither of us was very good at writing to the other. Then Harry started to express his feelings in his letters to me. They were very emotional and very loving. I didn't know what on earth was going on. I was married to somebody who was incredibly closed. Now he was opening up to me in a way he'd never done before.

I wasn't sure whether to believe it or not. I was fearful that I was being lifted up one minute, only to be dumped the next. Although Harry seemed to be enjoying the flow of the weekend, I found myself struggling. Here was the man I had married saying all these sweet things for the first time. Now he wanted to be with me, I wasn't sure I wanted to be with him.

Harry persisted with his letters and, somehow, I allowed them to soften my heart and penetrate my defensive outer shell.

***

The couples who were leading the course knew that we were struggling. But they gently encouraged us to stick at it.

Eventually we had this wonderful breakthrough moment. Kate wrote to me about how scared she was of trusting me, of venturing out of the self-protective prison that she had built for herself. But here she was. I wrote to her about how much I wanted to love her, about showing her the vulnerable little boy inside. Here I was.

Until then, I had loved Kate in my own disconnected way, with little more than a comfortable sense of affection and contentment. Now I actually felt real love. Both of us had risked opening ourselves up. Both of us had made ourselves deeply vulnerable. Now we were able to see each other free of the emotional masks that we wore to cover up our hidden fears and inadequacies.

It was an incredibly intimate moment. I've always said it's the moment I fell in love with my wife properly, for the first time, a mere nine years into our married life.

When we got back from the weekend, glowing, Kate bought me a wedding ring. It bears the dates of our original wedding and of that weekend. Ever since, we've been able to celebrate two anniversaries each year.

John and Adrienne are one of many hundreds of couples who came on a one-day course that we ran for couples getting married.

John hadn't really wanted to come in the first place. He had assumed it would be a boring waste of a day, more so as he was likely to miss the start of the England rugby match on television that afternoon. Even if it wasn't going to be boring, he imagined it would be embarrassing having to spend the day listening to other people's happy stories or tales of woe. Yuck.

Adrienne wanted to come for the sake of their relationship. Although she loved John, she knew that neither of them was heading into married life with a clean past. Both had had previous relationships; neither had had an ideal childhood. Although she hadn't quite dragged John along kicking and screaming, she had had to work hard to persuade him that the course was a good idea. She wanted to find out just how much they didn't already know about each other. Her biggest fear was about digging around in her past.

Neither of them should have worried. They finished the day feeling enthusiastic and glad they had come. John especially appreciated the fact that we cut short the lunch break in order to finish early. He caught the beginning of his rugby match.

We spoke to them a year or so later, after they had got married.

Adrienne said the main thing she'd learned on the course was that it was safe to disagree. After a childhood where open conflict was frowned upon, she found this liberating. It was OK to voice her strong opinions and argue with her husband, yet still love him enough to stay married for the rest of her life. She'd also benefited from one of the communication exercises, where she had to listen to John and then paraphrase what he'd just said back to him in her own words. It made her realize that, in her rush to say what she thought, she missed a lot of what John was saying. It had taken the sting out of some of the difficult discussions they'd subsequently had, such as about when to have children. Had she not done the course, she said, their marriage would have been different.

John said he'd learned one big thing from the course. Until that time, it had simply never occurred to him that he and Adrienne might want to be loved in different ways. There had been a number of occasions previously when he'd felt frustrated that his efforts to please her had fallen on stony ground. He was doing so much for her and yet all she would say was "I just want you to hang out with me". Since then, he had tried a new thing after work. Instead of disappearing off straight away to get on with some of the jobs that needed doing around the house, he regularly made them both a cup of tea, sat down, and asked her about her day. This ritual had become a central part of their married life. Now when he had to go away with his work, he really missed these special times together.

***

Well, that was all of fifteen years ago. John and Adrienne are still happily married and have three gorgeous children. Statistically speaking, staying married for fifteen years means that their risk of divorce has dropped from 40 per cent on their wedding day to a lowly 13 per cent now. So they are doing well!

Their story – and many others that we know – is a long way from proof that what they learned on a marriage course saved their marriage or made it stronger than it might otherwise have been. But their story fits with a wider body of evidence.

Great marriage can be learned.

Since the early 1980s, researchers have been observing and recording how couples deal with difficult issues, coding their patterns of behaviour, and seeing how those patterns influence who does well and who does badly years later.

One famous researcher, Professor John Gottman, claimed that he could predict from these patterns with up to 94 per cent accuracy who would still be together several years later.[1] These claims have since been shown to be somewhat exaggerated. The magic formula that works so well for one group of couples doesn't work nearly as well for a different group.[2] (This is actually quite a relief when you think about it. Otherwise, we could simply look at a couple and tell them "Well done, guys. You're a sure thing" or "Guys, give up now. Cancel the wedding. Your marriage is doomed.")

However – and it is a big "however" – the general principle that Professor Gottman applies is a good one. The seeds of our success and failure as a couple tomorrow can be seen – at least to some extent – in the way we get on with each other today. Couples who do well tend to have certain early characteristics in common. Likewise with couples who do less well. Fourteen years is the longest period we've seen this idea tested in a study.[3]

So what are these characteristics?[4]

It's undoubtedly the case that the way we are brought up influences the way we go on to live our life. Our family background, the way we were parented, our level of education, the family income: these are all factors that still affect the way we relate to others. But these "static" factors are hard or impossible to change because they have already happened.

It is also the case that how we view the world and how we behave affect the way we relate to others. These "dynamic" factors are a lot more open to change. We have a lot more choice. For example, if our practical communication skills as a couple are poor, or if we show contempt for one another, or if we think about divorce a lot, then our relationships are more likely to end in tears.

What marriage courses, relationship courses, and marriage preparation courses attempt to do is teach couples about the attitudes and practical skills that researchers have shown to be linked to future success and failure among couples.

Do courses work? Yes.

Yet it needs to be said that research in this field is difficult. The ideal study would gather a large group of couples together, split them in half, and tell one half of the couples to do the course and the other not. It's not going to happen! Therefore, most studies tend to rely on comparing those who have done a course with those who haven't. The obvious criticism is then that the kind of people who do courses were going to do better anyway, even if there's never been much hard evidence for this.[5]

Nonetheless, the best studies show that the best courses do appear to make a difference.[6] Even among newly-weds, who are a happy group to begin with, subsequent relationship satisfaction and commitment tends to be even higher, conflict even lower, and divorce even less common after they have done a pre-marriage course.[7] In one major study of military couples that did manage to use random assignment, already married couples who did the course – especially the more vulnerable ones – were half as likely to divorce within the next two years as couples who hadn't.[8]

***

Over the last twenty years or so, we've run hundreds of courses for thousands of couples, parents, prison families, young offenders… and top lawyers. Our own short programme, Let's Stick Together (for new parents), is now being run nationally by the charity Care for the Family.[9]

Any good course should cover three things:

- Good habits that make relationships work well;

- Bad habits that undermine relationships;

- Our attitude to one another and how it lies at the root of everything.

The rest of this chapter covers just a few of the typical ideas you might find on a course. You can put them into practice yourselves right now. But we hope you'll take the time and effort to go on a course. You'll get so much more out of it. Google "marriage course", or "marriage preparation course", or "relationship course", along with the town or county where you live, and see what comes up.

So what sort of thing do these courses cover?

Communication

It won't be much of a surprise to find that, if you ask people for the secret of a great relationship, the word "communication" comes up pretty quickly.[10]

Communication ought to be straightforward because there's so little involved. Tom needs to talk to Jenny about an important matter. He knows what he wants to tell her. There's a "message" in his brain that he has to "transmit" through his mouth. The message then passes through the "environment", where Jenny "receives" it in her ear and then "interprets" it in her own brain.

The process is so simple. What could possibly go wrong? And yet it so obviously does!

There are three main things that interfere with our communication:

- Tom doesn't say what he really means.

- Jenny doesn't interpret what she hears.

- The message gets lost somewhere between the two of them.

Learning how to spot signs of interference is an example of bad habits to avoid. Here are four of them:

- *I'm just not very interested in this subject.* Even if what you're saying seems really boring, I need to change my attitude and show interest. What's important to you should be important to me. Otherwise, my lack of interest will come across to you as if *you* are not very interesting to me. This is less a communication problem than an attitude problem.

- *I'm distracted.* My attention is elsewhere, whether it's the children crying or pressure at work or the TV programme I'm watching. This happens a lot. If I'm thinking about something else, I can't focus on you until whatever it is comes to an end. So it's good to have a general strategy that starts with saying what's going on: "I really want to hear what you've got to say. Can it wait until this has finished?"

- *I'm still feeling hurt from the last time we tried to discuss this.* Once again, I need to say what I need, which is that we stay gentle with one another while we try to discuss this.

- *I'm focused on myself because I'm Hungry, Angry, Lonely, or Tired (HALT).* Whenever our emotions are fired up, it can be really hard to pay attention to anything anyone says. Some people simply can't talk until their blood-sugar levels are restored with food. In our house, we have an expression called "panic tired", which is a signal to stop talking about anything! When our children were little, we used to have a daily moratorium on any kind of conversation – and an amnesty if either of us snapped – during the half-hour or so it took to de-stress after putting them to bed. It gave us a chance to calm down. Each of these is an example of taking a "time-out", the big trick of which is to make sure we "time in" again, for example when I'm no longer quite as Hungry, Angry, Lonely, or Tired.

Spend a few moments thinking which of these interferes with your listening to your spouse or partner.

***

Love

Assumptions are the enemy of healthy relationships.

The biggest assumption of all surrounds commitment. Couples can live together for years without ever having an open and honest conversation about how they each see their future together. When those hidden plans don't match up, the more committed person can spend their life treading on eggshells, anxious to avoid a confrontation that might cause their loved one to walk out. In sharp contrast, the less committed person can behave with impunity because, ultimately, they don't really care whether they stay or go.

We've already told you the tragic, and all too common, story of Peter and Elena. His affair happened because he had never fully bought into their life together – even though they had got married. Teaching them how to communicate a bit better might have helped them survive for a little longer. But it wouldn't have dealt with the underlying problem of his indifferent attitude to their relationship. Elena had assumed he was as committed as she was.

Until the day his affair was unmasked, they had never actually had a serious conversation to clarify their plans for the future. Had they done so before the wedding train gathered its unstoppable head of steam, they might either have resolved their dilemma and gone ahead with a deeper understanding of one another, or never have married in the first place.

But even when, as a couple, we are on the same page of commitment, we can also be on very different pages of love. We are equally committed. We both love each other. Yet neither of us feels loved.

The **Five Love Languages**, identified by psychologist Gary Chapman, are one of the simplest and most accessible ideas used by marriage courses.[11] We adapted it slightly for Let's Stick Together [12] and will describe the way we use it here.

The big assumption here is that I assume that the way I most naturally show love to you is the way you most want to receive it. What works for me will work for you. Only it almost always doesn't. It's as if I speak French and assume you will understand. You reply in Chinese and assume I will understand.

We both love each other. Yet neither of us feels loved. We need to learn and speak each other's love language.

In our version of this, the five languages are Time, Words, Actions, Gifts, and Touch. As we go through them, try to identify your own preferred language or languages. Most people tend to have one or two that stand out. You may like all of them, or none. There is no right or wrong here.

Time people like hanging out with others. If time is my love language, then I love it when a friend or loved one spends time with me. Maybe we just hang out in the kitchen over a coffee. Maybe we go and watch a film together. They don't have to say very much or do very much. But it feels as if they care enough to give me their time. For me, time is love. They could be spending it with anyone else, but they are choosing to spend it with me. Having somebody around therefore makes me feel appreciated, recognized, connected; a valued part of the human race. It feels good. And because time is the way I most feel loved, then hanging out with friends and family is probably the most natural and easy way for me to show I love them. I don't have to do much or say much. I'm simply showing that I care because I am there with them. Hanging out makes me a time person.

Words people love it when a friend or loved one chats with us about life, what's going on, anything. This is more than just hanging out. It's the chatting that is important here. Sharing what's going on in our lives makes me feel connected, valued, special. And because words is my love language, it probably comes easily and naturally to me to want to chat to others. This is my way of expressing affection, connection, love. There are other aspects of words that may or may not be important to me. It could be that the way I'm spoken to is especially important: gentleness and kindness say everything. Or it could be that being appreciated or affirmed or complimented on how I look or what I've done is especially important: I love being noticed and I also find it easy to be complimentary to others. Or it could be that encouragement about the future is what does it for me: I am a natural encourager. Chatting, encouraging, complimenting, or just being kind in the way I speak makes me a words person.

Actions people love it when a friend or loved one does something for us or with us. Actions speak louder than words. It might be a particular type of action that really emphasizes this. Somebody takes on a chore that I would otherwise have to do myself: changing the baby's nappy, doing the family shopping, emptying the bin, making the bed, doing the washing up. It could be an action that makes me feel cared for: cooking me dinner, giving me a lift, running my bath. Or it might be a job that makes me feel supported: organizing the car repair or the family holiday, fixing the broken sink, putting up a shelf. Alternatively, it could be doing things together that makes me feel loved, such as going on a bike ride or a walk together, or playing sports or games together. It's most likely that the action or activity I appreciate most is also what I find it easiest to do for others. Doing things for or with others makes me an actions person.

Gifts people love it when a friend or loved one gives us a little something: a note, a card, a trinket, a chocolate bar, a flower. It shows they've been thinking about us. With gifts, it's very much the thought that counts. Expensive presents are all very well, but the love language of gifts is not about the expense. Little is often all it takes. Somebody has spent time thinking about me. They've given me a diary in the particular format I wanted, or my favourite flowers, or a sympathetic note. If that's the kind of thing I do naturally for others, I'm a gifts person.

Touch people feel loved when somebody gives us a hug, or holds our hand, or touches us on the shoulder. There's something about physical contact that conveys love and affection to me; I feel accepted, secure, loved. It helps me feel more open and warm. Touch doesn't mean sex, although clearly sex meets the same need. Touch is how I convey love: a hug for my spouse when I see him/ her after work, a hand on my friend's shoulder. If I do it to others without thinking, it makes me a touch person.

Learning about love languages before they got married helped John and Adrienne – whom we met earlier in this chapter – understand a lot better what made each other tick.

Realizing that his wife just wanted him to hang out and chat with her, John discovered that his marriage went a whole lot better when he remembered to sit down after work and ask about her day. It was a chance for them to connect that was especially important to her. He learned that Adrienne is a Words person. She feels loved and appreciated when John chats with her. Even though John had to make a deliberate decision to do this every day at first – rather than disappearing off to get on with other things – their daily chats have now become an automatic ritual that they both love.

Realizing that her husband wanted to do things to bless her, Adrienne made a big effort to do the same for him. She learned that John is an Actions person. Although, as the better cook, John had originally assumed responsibility for most of the cooking during their early days together, he really appreciated the effort Adrienne made to take over from time to time. She also made a point of organizing anything to do with sport for John. These are two simple ways that show John how much she loves him.

Had they never heard about love languages, it's quite likely that their marriage might have suffered from all sorts of unnecessary misunderstandings.

The truly extraordinary thing is that hardly any couple share the same love languages. According to Harry's study of new parents, only 6 per cent of couples had exactly the same combination.[13] Even more remarkably, there was only a one-in-four chance that their spouse or partner shared their main love language.

Once you've figured out what makes you feel loved – your own love language – then ask your spouse or partner what they think theirs is. You might be surprised. Then suggest some things you could do for or with them using that language, and do it.

Remember that the most important thing is not to assume. Check!

***

Time

Time is the oxygen of friendship. Without time spent together, no friendship will get off the ground. Without time spent together, even the best of friendships will inevitably decay. No wonder many relationship courses enthusiastically promote the idea of date nights as a way of keeping the love alive.

Harry and Steve McKay's recent study of date nights for Marriage Foundation is probably the first analysis of its kind anywhere in the world. They found that parents with young children who said they went out once a month as a couple were more likely to still be together ten years later compared to those who hardly ever went out as a couple. This was only true for married couples and not for unmarried couples. It was also true regardless of how happy couples were with their marriage at the time.[14]

The interesting thing about this study is that only married couples gain this extra benefit. What seems to be happening is that if couples are already committed, an occasional "date night" reinforces that commitment. It's part of the long term plan to make their relationship work. If couples are less committed, date night has no effect. It's just a night out.

A host of studies emphasize the overall importance of spending quality time together, especially when you are parents. For example:

- A US study of dual-earning working-class couples found that wives who reported more shared time together before becoming parents also reported more marital love and less conflict at their child's first birthday. The opposite was true if husbands spent more time on their own before becoming parents.[15]

- A UK study of working fathers found that those who worked at weekends made up for time lost with their children during the week. But they did not do this with their wife or partner.[16]

- Another US study found that the decline in relationship quality commonly experienced by new mothers could be explained by spending less time together as a couple – and also by the perception of increased unfairness in housework.[17]

It is time spent together that builds a friendship. With it, friendships thrive. Without it, they decay.

Tom and Anne were childhood sweethearts. They had first met as teenagers at school, and by the time they had finished university, they were married. Each of them began to build their own career, Tom in a company that provided airport services, Anne as a teacher. By the time Anne became pregnant with their first child, they were both in their early thirties. Tom was doing well enough at work for them to agree that Anne should step back from her career for at least her first year as a mother.

By the time that first year of motherhood was over, Anne was pregnant again. She loved being a mother and liked having the freedom not to have to work. But, as the children grew older and started at nursery school, Anne began to feel increasingly lonely at home. When Tom wasn't working long hours at his main office, he was travelling around the world on business.

In the evenings and at weekends, he would return exhausted and flop. There was little time for them as a couple. Even when chatting, he would glaze over after five minutes and put the television on.

Tom was undoubtedly generous. To the outside world, it looked as if she had nothing to complain about. Her husband gave her gifts, a new watch, a smart car, a cleaner for their home.

In short, she had everything. Except him.

Anne tried talking to Tom many times over the years. But each time he would react defensively, asking why all the things he provided for her weren't enough. Defeated, but still in love with Tom, she got back into teaching. Part-time work at least made her feel valued as more than "just a mum". Anne became resigned to a marriage that gave her a comfortable life but left her empty inside. She lived in hope that something would change. Yet, no matter what she said, it didn't.

Their children were well into their primary school years when a work friend announced to Tom over lunch that he was getting a divorce. Tom was shocked to hear that it was his friend's wife who had pushed him out. Long hours and business trips had apparently taken their toll. His friend's wife said she had felt lonely at home. The years had passed and her resolve to stay married to an absent husband was gradually worn away. Eventually somebody had shown interest in her and she succumbed to the temptation. The marriage was over.

That night, over a typically late dinner, Tom told Anne about his colleague. "What I can't understand is that he did everything for her. What more could he have done?" There wasn't even a hint of irony as he completely failed to recognize his own situation mirrored in theirs.

Anne laid it out for him. "I understand her. She's me. That's how I feel. You leave early and come home late. It's not much of a life. The only difference is that I haven't had an affair. Yet."

For the first time, the words sank in. Tom realized the mistake he'd made. Being a provider was in his blood. But it dawned on him that he'd been taking Anne for granted. Over the next few weeks, Tom began to see the world from Anne's point of view for the first time. He softened his attitude towards her and was a lot more attentive, realizing that merely being a good provider was not making her happy.

Tom still worked his long hours. But now he made time for Anne where before he hadn't. He made a point of having lunch with her at least once during the week. Rather than collapse onto a sofa in front of the television at weekends, he prioritized whatever she wanted to do. Usually, that meant time with him as well as with the children. And he even turned down unnecessary trips overseas, where before he wouldn't have thought twice about going.

These changes allowed Anne to say to a friend that, for the first time since they'd had children, she felt happily married.

***

Now find yourselves a course. Take the time to do it together. And stay happily married!

For better, for worse

"For better" is the easy bit. A survey carried out for this book shows that almost all happy couples have been through bad patches. Nationally, almost all unhappy couples will stay together. They tend to do that by changing circumstances, working it out, or making a decision to stick it out. Newly-wed couples and parents tell us how they have got through bad patches. Harry and Kate recount some of their own bad moments.

Here's a question for you if you're married.

Think back to the day you made your vows: "For better, for worse; for richer, for poorer; in sickness and in health, to love and to cherish, till death us do part."

Did you ever, even for one second, actually focus on the "worse, poorer, sickness" bit?

Of course you didn't. Nor did we. Maybe nobody ever does. But we'd guess that you've thought about those vows a lot more in the subsequent years.

Unless you are very unusual, you'll have had difficult times together as a couple, times when it's hard to love one another, to respect one another, even to be nice to one another; times when you're cross with one another, or you're just not communicating properly with one another.

You love each other. But you don't like each other.

Half of the couples in our survey who said they were happy in their relationship right now also said they had been unhappy at some point. One in six of today's happy couples even said they had been very unhappy at some time. We were in that latter category.

Bad times come for all sorts of reasons. Couples lose focus and drift apart, as we did. Couples experience times of change that put them under a great deal of pressure, such as bereavement or losing a job. To us, the most obviously difficult time in any marriage is when you have small children.

Recently some friends arrived to stay at our house with their three little ones. We watched in awe as they got all their stuff unpacked while juggling tired children. The kitchen then became a hive of activity as they shovelled food into ever-so-fractious mouths. While we cleared up behind them, mum went off to read one of the children a story while dad took two of them upstairs for a bath. They then swapped roles for a while before finally getting all three down to sleep. It was exhausting just watching them!

How on earth do they cope, we asked one another. How on earth do lone parents cope with just the one pair of hands? Then we looked at each other before wondering how we managed it with six children.

The answer is that we didn't cope all the time. Leaving aside the major crisis that almost brought us down as a couple, we had some other pretty bad moments along the way.

All relationships run in cycles.

If you think about this for a moment, you will realize that a cycle of ups and downs is completely normal and natural. In fact, cycles are inevitable. The idea of a "stable relationship" is nonsense.

Relationships can be secure, but they cannot be stable. They must always be cyclical.

When one of us is nice to the other, it's a whole lot easier for the other person to be nice in return. When they are nice to us, we are more likely to be nice back. And so on. It's a virtuous spiral where the positives feed off each other.

On the other hand, when one of us is not so nice, or forgets to be nice, it becomes harder for the other person to be nice back. They might not be outright unpleasant, but our lack of niceness might tempt them into becoming a little more closed off or resentful. At the very least, they may stop being nice. Faced with somebody who is then less nice to us, it then becomes a little bit harder for us to be nice in return. And so on. This time, it's a vicious spiral where the negatives feed off each other.

Some couples experience the cycle of ups and downs as a series of waves. They could be big stormy tempestuous waves if couples are emotional and hot-headed. One moment they are at each other hammer and tongs, the next locked in a passionate embrace. You see this in the movies. The protagonists gaze into each other's eyes and, all of a sudden, war and hate become peace and love. How did that happen?! Rather more marriages resemble a long slow swell where couples are more chilled, relaxed, and easy-going. Cycles are less pronounced, less dramatic. The turning points are less obvious.

Our own cycle of ups and downs is more like the blips you see on a heart monitor. Long periods of calm followed by a sudden crash!

We sometimes think of it as a journey across a glacier. High up on an Antarctic mountain range, the air is clear and fresh. There's beautiful and dramatic scenery all around. The snow and ice make us feel alive. It's an exciting and challenging adventure. But a glacier is also a dangerous place, dotted with crevasses that will swallow us up if we lose concentration. We need to work as a team.

Our downward cycle happens when we start to enjoy the

adventure on our own a bit too much. We forget the safety rules and allow ourselves to let go of one another. Almost imperceptibly, we start to drift apart. Both of us are aware that this is happening. But life is good; big family life means there is plenty to do. We try not to let it worry us.

At some point we notice that we are too far apart for safety. Yet neither wants to admit it. Other priorities allow us to ignore the growing sense of danger. Our cries for help tend to focus on our own needs rather than on supporting one another. Sooner or later some little issue triggers an argument, and we fall suddenly and shockingly into a deep, dark crevasse. It feels scary and alone. Well and truly stuck in this difficult and uncomfortable situation, eventually one of us summons the courage to initiate the rescue mission. It seems like a huge task. Yet, like the warring couple in the movies who inexplicably stop to kiss and make up, the extraordinary thing is how quickly we can get back on track and start working as a team again.

Because our six children were born over a period of twelve years, Harry and I have spent a very large part of our marriage managing small people in our big family. It has, of course, been utterly wonderful watching them grow and mature into the capable, independent, and quite different teens and young adults that they are now. It feels as if we are in a season of reward for all those years of exhaustion. It was indeed just a phase.

But the long season of exhaustion occasionally hit some especially low points that put huge pressure on our marriage. Perhaps our most difficult moment was when I was pregnant with our fifth child. Imagine running a household with four children aged one, three, seven, and nine. It was quite enough of a challenge for two fully fit adults. Harry and I work well as a team. But then, as I became larger, I became progressively less and less capable.

One day, Harry started to go down with a cold, so I despatched him into the countryside for a twenty-mile walk in the hills. I thought the fresh air and exercise would revitalize him. Instead, he came back with a high temperature and full-blooded pneumonia. He spent the next month flat on his back in bed.

Unable to cope on my own, I put out a cry for help to our local church, who were amazing. They fed our entire family for the whole of the next month. But even though I knew Harry was seriously ill, I began to feel resentful that he was lying uselessly in bed while I and my large tummy were struggling to get the children bathed, clothed, fed, and schooled on my own.

***

I don't think I've ever felt so hopeless in all my life. This wasn't just an exaggerated case of man flu; it was full-blown pneumonia. I could see how shattering it was for Kate, but there was little I could do. Any time I got out of bed, I felt shivery and weak, barely able to walk from our bedroom.

Thankfully, these things eventually blow over. My amazing wife survived. Our church family were hugely supportive. I got better. And our fifth child was born.

There was now a desperate need for us to spend proper time together and focus on one another as a couple. We had been in survival mode for too long and needed to restore our friendship.

So, when a group of old friends from our time overseas suggested a reunion dinner, we jumped at the chance of a night out on our own without the children.

Almost the best part of it was that it was going to be a two-hour journey to get there. So, with the prospect of lots of lovely time to chat, we headed off in our van – we were long past being able to fit our big family into a normal car.

Within fifteen minutes of leaving the house, we fell straight into a crevasse.

***

Unbelievable. After all these months of barely coping, at last we had a chance to talk.

I can't even remember what sparked the row. It was probably some little thing that I wanted Harry to acknowledge. But he just wouldn't say sorry. I didn't feel understood and became more and more angry. Harry kept saying he needed to concentrate on driving and seemed to shut down. The argument went round in circles for the full length of the journey.

I put on a brave face for my friends at the restaurant. Then we got back into the van for another two hours of miscommunication and hurt on the way home.

I had been so looking forward to our lovely evening together. It had felt like a transition point where we could rediscover each other once again. Instead, it couldn't have gone any worse.

***

I have no idea how it all went so wrong.

It's probably not the best idea to have a deep and meaningful discussion when you're also concentrating on driving along the motorway. My attention was divided and I couldn't exactly look her in the eye. I missed something important Kate said, and then compounded my error by failing to back down or apologize. I know it's one of the excuses I play over in my mind when I can't work out what to apologize for. The journey there and back was awful.

In the morning, I decided we needed to call on some lovely friends of ours, Arthur and Jenny, who are a little older and a lot wiser.

Jenny answered the phone. "Can we come over and see you?" I squeaked. Bearing in mind that they lived even further away, the prospect of another long and frosty journey might not have been the best idea. Nonetheless, Jenny agreed graciously. She also seemed surprised that we needed their help.

"Surely you should know what to do by now?" she said. After all, I taught courses on relationships.

"I know," I mumbled sheepishly. "It's not working,"

Just before we rang off, Jenny asked me whether I was spending time with Kate. It was like a light bulb going on. I said thank you and hung up. The error of my ways was suddenly all too apparent.

We didn't just need time together. We needed to re-establish our friendship. I needed to look Kate in the eye, tell her how amazing she was, and give her 100 per cent of my concentration. When I was driving, I couldn't do that. I couldn't catch every little nuance. Instead of acknowledging what she said, I took it personally and became defensive. Kate needed her friend.

Later that evening, we sat together on our bed for three hours, looking into each other's eyes, chatting about everything and nothing. We did what friends do. We reconnected.

As if by magic, we found ourselves back up on that beautiful glacier, enjoying the view together. We were out of the crevasse. The heart monitor had pinged its sign of life once again.

Our marriage was back on track.

At first glance, Jason and Melissa fit the typical stereotype of a hard-working married couple with two children, now aged ten and nine. They also differ from many couples both in personality and in the way they have swapped home and work roles.

Their story is inspiring, however, because they illustrate the importance of love, pragmatism, and perseverance through the same challenging phase of family life with young children and in how they cope with their own differences. They are a little behind us in that, as their children get older and become more self-sufficient, they are only now beginning to emerge into the sunshine once again. Their future is bright.

Role reversal is one way Jason and Melissa differ from most couples. Unsurprisingly, for their first two years as parents, Melissa put her career as a pharmacist on hold in order to be a mum at home. Although she loved her children, she quickly realized that she needed the intellectual stimulation and challenge of getting back into work. A return to part-time work suited her well. The extra income also helped them as they were struggling to stay on top of their bills.

As an office manager in a company that was losing its way, Jason saw the writing on the wall. So, when he lost his job, they were well prepared. Melissa had previously sounded out her employer about taking on a full-time role. Jason prepared himself for the job of full-time father.

The transition was seamless. One day, Melissa was doing most of the childcare and shopping. The next day, Jason took over. At first it felt to Jason as if he was on holiday. He would plan the food for the family and pop off to the shops to buy the ingredients. He loved cooking. While running the house, children, and cooking, Jason also found himself a new part-time role with a different company.

Melissa's new full-time post was as rewarding as she had hoped. But being on her feet all day was also exhausting. Melissa made the assumption that when Jason took over at home, he would run the family in the same way she had done. But, like any two human beings, they were different.

Jason was a natural at playing with the children, cooking them a wide variety of healthy foods, and getting them to school on time. Where he fell short was in the mess that he left behind. Tidying up behind him was never a priority. To him, getting all these other things done was far more important. The mess could always be sorted out later.

When Melissa returned home from a long day at work, what she needed was a tidy, clean house to help her calm down. Instead, all she could see was the mess. To her, clothes left lying around and washing up still in the sink meant chaos. It made her feel very uncomfortable in her own home.

She resented the fact that Jason didn't seem to care that a tidy house meant the world to her. It left her feeling increasingly angry. She would churn the same thought over and over in her mind. Jason was inconsiderate. He put his own priorities in front of what she wanted and needed.

Then one day, in the middle of a routine grump about the state of the house, it dawned on her. Jason was amazingly considerate to her, just not in the way she most wanted. He made her lunch and took it across town if she forgot it. He would come out to collect her after a long day behind the counter of the pharmacy, to save her taking the bus. He planned special days out for her and the children. He loved organizing holidays. He wanted to cook her amazing food.

Her solution was to accept that tidying the house was not Jason's thing. For whatever reason, it was a bridge too far for him. She'd just have to do it herself, which she now does. Of course, it's not ideal. She still has to come home to the mess. But things are now more peaceful between them.

Interestingly, Jason and Melissa have not only swapped roles but are also more like the opposite stereotype as regards personality.

Jason is an extrovert who wants conversation and loves to do things as a family. During the day, he texts Melissa at work to keep in touch. When she comes home, he wants to chat with her and hang out. Jason also loves food and cooking. He loves planning adventures for them as a family. He thinks his plans and variety are a way of loving his family.

Melissa, on the other hand, is an introvert. Because she has to deal with people all day long, she admits to not thinking about family at all when she is at work. When she gets home, the one thing she needs is peace and quiet. It's her way of regaining energy. Unlike Jason, she's not at all interested in cooking and is a lot less adventurous with menu planning. She's a home bird who wants to do very little when she's not working and would happily eat the same food every week.

Jason finds this very frustrating and feels low on her list of priorities. It's possible that his unwillingness to tidy up for her – while showing love in so many other ways – is his little act of rebellion.

Both Jason and Melissa are completely exhausted. They work long hours. Now that the children are well established in primary school, Jason has also taken a full-time job. Because he has a little more flexibility, he steps up and takes over if the children are ill.

But they both also recognize that they are in a difficult phase of life. In two years, both children will be at secondary school, be older and more independent, and need less childcare. It's a phase.

Jason and Melissa are a really good example of a couple who live out the "for better, for worse" part of their vows wonderfully well. Maybe their personalities were particularly well suited to role change. Whatever the reason, they had a sufficiently strong friendship to be able to foresee the loss of Jason's job and come up with a pragmatic solution.

Yet the real hero of this story is not who you might think.

The way Jason dealt with his new role as a stay-at-home dad

makes him in some ways a perfect role model. He loved his children and got the job done. He also showed his love for his wife in running spontaneous errands for her and planning their life together.

Yet, somewhere along the line, he couldn't quite bring himself to put her first in the way she most needed.

What was most important to Melissa was order and cleanliness. Yes, he was – and is – a brilliant dad. Children were his first priority. But his second priority was not Melissa, but himself. Instead of spending a few extra minutes each day doing the necessary but boring chores that would most have blessed his wife, he chose to spend his time having fun and cooking with the children.

This might all seem a bit picky. After all, many mothers would give their right arm to have a husband who is that good with the children and caring enough to come and collect them from work. But, as our survey found, the number-one priority for mums is not children. It's friendship. And, although Jason and Melissa have bucked the trend by reversing roles, the number-one area where mums would like a little more contribution is in the domestic chores.

Melissa told Jason enough times what she needed, what would bless her. He chose not to respond. He's still a good man. He loves and cares for Melissa in lots of other ways. She knows that.

Ultimately, it's Melissa who is the star of the show. It was her little shift in attitude that allowed her to focus on Jason the amazing dad rather than Jason the not entirely considerate husband. It was her perseverance and her sacrifice that have allowed them to ride out this difficult phase of married life.

Some will call this give and take. Actually, they are both big givers. It makes them a wonderful couple, who have a bright future.

***

What is it that helps couples get through bad patches?

We think it's the big picture of how we see one another. When we see something that has a lot of value, we tend to treat it differently from something that has less value. So when we think of our spouse (and our marriage) as especially valuable for his or her own sake, we ought to treat him or her with more care.

Let's have a look at an example of how this works in a different setting.

A woman who owns some nice costume jewellery is likely to feel relaxed about wearing it at a party. Because it wasn't expensive when she bought it, she will put it on without a great deal of thought, other than that she likes wearing it. If it were ever damaged or lost, it probably wouldn't bother her that much. For now, she likes it. But her overall attitude to it is ambivalent.

Now imagine an identical piece of jewellery that is real – worth thousands, if not more. She's going to view this very differently. She will be careful about how and where she wears it. She will treat it with much more care, double-checking the clasp several times during an evening, nervous in case it falls off or gets stolen.

The two pieces of jewellery look and feel the same. But because the latter has a lot more value, it profoundly affects the way the woman views and treats it.

Back to marriage again. There's some really interesting research on the main ways in which couples view marriage and their spouse. Brad Wilcox and Jeffrey Dew at the University of Virginia have found that couples tend to embrace either a "soulmate" or an "institutional" model of marriage.[1]

Those who buy into the "soulmate" idea of marriage are essentially saying "Follow your heart". There's one person out there who makes you feel utterly wonderful. They complete you. You are empty without them. They are your other half. At the core of a strong marriage is the kind of passionate love that can only come from a "soulmate".

In contrast, those who buy into the "institutional" idea of marriage – what a ghastly word, but bear with us – are essentially saying "Follow your head". When you got married, you bought into a plan for your life together and that's what's going to happen. Your spouse and your marriage have value in their own right. It's not so much a gushing kind of love that matters most but a deep love that comes from commitment and belonging. Your marriage is part of a bigger picture that affects, and is influenced by, those around you.

Needless to say, the "soulmate" group tend to have more volatile marriages, with high levels of satisfaction but also high levels of conflict and divorce. In other words, they are fun but unstable. The reason is straightforward. When you rely so much on feeling great, when you "follow your heart", you are ultimately relying on the other person to make you happy. When they have an inevitable day off from bringing you sweetness and light, it's going to put a dent in your marriage.

The "institutional" group have the opposite problem, but only if they are secular in outlook and have lower levels of social connection and support. While being relatively stable, they also tend to have lower levels of happiness. They have serious marriages, which hang on in there but don't seem to be much fun.

The couples who did best in this study tended to combine these two ideas. They viewed their marriage as important but also expressed themselves well to one another and were well embedded in a community. In this particular study, the community happened to be faith-based.

Either way, what this study is saying is that a "soulmate" kind of marriage, on its own, will end in tears. What matters is the big picture, how you value your marriage and each other.

In case you're sceptical about the religious angle, one of the best studies on how this affects marriage comes from Professor Annette Mahoney and colleagues at Bowling Green State University, Ohio.

Her studies show that it is not religious pursuits per se that make marriage work well; it's how you apply them. It wasn't the couples who went to church lots who did best; it was the couples who viewed their marriage as "God-inspired" or "sacred". In other words, they attached a particularly high value to their marriage.[2]

What we value with our heads will then make our hearts feel good. In other words, where you spend most of your time and energy is where your love is.

"*Where your treasure is, there your heart will be also*" (Matthew 6:21).

The key factor that helps couples through bad patches, like so much else in a marriage, boils down to dedication.

Dedication is that powerful combination of

- making a decision

- to be a couple

- with a permanent future.

When you view your spouse and your marriage as the most important things, that attitude in your head will inevitably work its way down to your heart. If you've fallen out of love, it's because you've stopped valuing your marriage. Value your spouse and you will feel the love come back.

I love you and want to be close to you

In the early years of marriage, couples tend to cope with an absence of kindness. What causes problems is the presence of unkindness. This can show itself in bad habits that can become entrenched. We call them STOP signs: Scoring points, Thinking the worst, Opting out, Putting down. Harry and Kate are no exception. One issue plagued them more than any other. Their problem – and solution – will resonate with many couples. The result, twenty-eight years into their marriage, was their happiest year yet!

Thus far in the book, we've talked a lot about the importance of family life, how to make it work better, and how the way we see each other and our marriage makes the biggest difference.

But, even with the best will in the world, things can still go wrong for the simple reason that we are fallible human beings. We blow it. We have arguments. We're selfish.

We all get tired. We all get grumpy. We're all far from perfect. And we all come with our own baggage that makes us react in unhelpful ways. We say things we don't mean. We treat one another in ways we shouldn't.

On their own, we can laugh off those little things. We have a big-picture view of our marriage. We're in this for the long haul.

We say to ourselves, "Kate – or Harry – is just having a bad day at the office." We can then attribute our spouse's grumpiness to some other factor. The big picture tells us that our spouse is a good person who loves us. So this bad reaction must be due to something else, whether it's pressure at work, not feeling well, the time of the month, or being worried about something.

What we have to watch out for is when we start attributing these odd bouts of bad behaviour to them as a person. It's not their circumstances; it's who they are. He or she is erratic, prickly, grumpy, unkind, bad-tempered. This thought process then becomes a slippery slope. We begin to lose sight of the big picture and get more and more focused on what's going wrong.[1]

Arguments can happen over any subject where couples have differences. The bigger the difference, the bigger the potential for argument. In surveys, people tend to say that money is their number-one cause of arguments.

Professor Lauren Papp of the University of Wisconsin-Madison, and colleagues, ran a detailed study of what couples actually argue about in real time. She asked 100 couples with children to keep a daily diary of arguments over a two-week period.[2]

By far the most common source of arguments turns out to be the children – how we parent them, spend time with them, nurture them, and deal with their behaviour. Well behind this come chores – our family and household responsibilities – and then communication – the way we speak and listen, what we said, and whether we felt heard and understood.

Trailing in fifth place, just behind arguments over how we spend our leisure time and issues related to work, comes money – how we earn it, spend it, and save it.

Yet although money may not be the most frequent topic of arguments, it tends to be the most stressful. Couples report that they argue for longer and with more intensity about money. These arguments are also the ones that are most likely to recur and least likely to be resolved.

Of course, when we argue about money, we're not really arguing about money itself. It's what money represents: our values, hopes, and fears, our willingness to trust and our need for control, our past and future, and our sense of identity: *"I am somebody if I have money"*; *"I am in control with money"*; *"I can trust my loved one with money"*; *"I have a secure future if I have money"*; *"I fear losing money"*.

So the way we discuss money matters as a couple really boils down to the way we argue. This in turn reflects these deeper issues of fear, power, control, and identity. When we realize this, it becomes more obvious that how we handle our differences is the key to a successful marriage. It's not the subject that matters so much. It's how we handle it.

In the Benson household, we are fortunate in that we almost never have arguments over money. We have similar views that life will work with or without money, and we also have a deep sense of trust in one another regarding the way we earn, spend, save, and treat money.

But we do have arguments about chores and the way we communicate differently. Once again, at root, these arguments are never really about chores or communication at all. They tend to be about much deeper matters, in our case expectations and passivity.

We suspect that "passivity" will ring bells with a lot of people – men in particular – because it's about the need for control. Passivity means doing things in our own time, which is pretty much the opposite of the active, attentive, and sacrificial mindset that characterizes a good marriage.

Although we have no direct evidence, the link with control suggests that passivity may well be more of a male problem. The need for control lies behind all sorts of social phenomena. At the trivial end of the scale is the popular stereotype that men don't ask for directions. At the extreme and serious end is why the kind of domestic abuse known as "intimate terrorism" invariably involves men controlling women.

We'll come back to this shortly.

***

In the chapter on "Learning to Love", we mentioned the famous American researcher Professor John Gottman. One of his most interesting findings is that what puts a marriage at risk in its early years is not a lack of love. It's the way we treat one another negatively that matters most.[3]

He describes these negative behaviours as "The Four Horsemen". This is a tumbling cascade of negativity where "Criticism" turns into "Defensiveness", which then creates "Contempt", and eventually "Stonewalling".[4]

"Criticism" points the finger at the person's character. The person under attack responds with "Defensiveness". This triggers an attitude of "Contempt" for failing to address the original problem. Communication then breaks down. Both sides "Stonewall" and withdraw from the conversation. Both are left hurt and the relationship is in trouble.

Another American research group, led by Professors Howard Markman and Scott Stanley, did similar research, identifying four "Danger Signs" that they called "Withdrawal", "Escalation", "Invalidation", and "Negative Interpretation".[5]

There's clearly a lot of overlap here with the "Four Horsemen". But, rather than presenting them as a cascade in which one leads inexorably to the other, their view was that any one of these four "Danger Signs" posed a risk to a relationship if not nipped in the bud.

Both sides have a point. But we think the wording could be made a lot easier to remember and understand. Not many people will have the presence of mind to stop themselves in the middle of an argument because they've suddenly realized, "Hey, I'm stonewalling here", or "I need to watch out for my negative interpretation". It's not going to happen, is it?!

And so we came up with the idea of "STOP signs", four little red flags that are easy to remember and which will hopefully also stop you in your tracks.

- **S = Scoring points.** This is when your argument descends into tit for tat: "You left your trousers on the floor, again." "What? Well, you left the dishes in the sink. Again." "OK, since we're getting it all out there now, you didn't book in the car like I asked you to. Nor did you post my letter." "Well, you're not so perfect, are you?" "If you don't like it, you're free to leave." And so on.

   Few people get out of bed deliberately thinking of ways to criticize or create conflict. This argument started with a complaint that was delivered badly and taken badly. A simple apology for leaving trousers lying around would have nipped this in the bud, thereby stopping an argument from escalating out of control and giving this couple a thoroughly unpleasant start to their day.

- **T = Thinking the worst.** This is when you stop taking things at face value and assume there's more to it than meets the eye. Perhaps you're in trouble or they're out to get you: *"He's bought me flowers. He never does that normally. What's he done wrong?"* *"He's being nice all of a sudden. I wonder what he* wants?" "She made herself a cup of tea this morning, but didn't make me one. What have I done to upset her?"

Just as with Scoring points, most people don't wake up in the morning with a hidden agenda that means they are out to get you. The usual reason why situations get misinterpreted is past experience. Maybe every time a teacher or parent spoke to you when you were a child, it was to criticize. Or maybe somebody treated you badly in a previous relationship. It's not surprising that, when faced with a similar comment, action, or tone, it triggers an old reaction that should no longer apply.

- **O = Opting out.** At some point in an argument, it all becomes too much. "Right, that's it," you say, getting up and leaving the room. The trouble is that walking away like this sends a message that you don't care. You don't want to deal with it. It's not important enough to you. You're no longer listening. You're blanking them.

  Some people find conflict at home really hard to deal with. The stress of the argument becomes too much. That might be OK if you make things clear: *"I'm not handling things very well at the moment. Give me a few minutes."* Once you've calmed down, you can try again. The trouble is that most of us don't take time-outs like this, which are healthy. We walk away and don't come back, closing the door on this topic. Make a habit of this and eventually so many doors are closed that there is no room for conversation and friendship. Not good.

- **P = Putting down.** And, finally, somebody does something that winds you up. The white van that nearly reverses into you. The parent who mistreats her child in the shop. The telephone call-centre employee who can't deal with your enquiry. Every bone in your body cries out "Moron!" You sigh in frustrated contempt. You roll your eyes. You utter the odd expletive.

This is all very well in situations that don't really matter. But don't do it at home. When you put somebody down, you are saying that they have less value than you. You are clever; they are stupid. Even if it's true, it's not a great way to run an intimate relationship between friends and lovers.

One of the most striking aspects of STOP signs is that they almost certainly reflect underlying insecurities and anxieties about the relationship. Patterns of negative behaviour are formed as one spouse or partner behaves badly and the other person reacts accordingly.

In chapter five, we talked about the well-known "demand–withdraw" phenomenon, where one spouse pursues the other over some injustice, and the other runs away. In terms of STOP signs, this is a toxic combination of Scoring points and Opting out that has long been linked with lower levels of marital satisfaction.[6]

Harry's study of the way new parents use STOP signs showed that this goes far beyond the stereotype of wives nagging and husbands hiding in their cave. Whereas only one in three couples fit the stereotype, two in three couples use "demand–withdraw" in some form or another.

A particular combination of these negative behaviours is also more common among unmarried cohabiting parents than among married ones, even after differing age or education levels have been taken into account. Among cohabiting parents, nearly half either both Opt out ("Back off") or the father Puts down and the mother then Thinks the worst as well as Scores points or Puts down in return ("Fire back"). This pattern of "Back off or Fire back" only occurs among one-quarter of married parents.[7]

People often wonder how the simple act of getting married makes a difference. This difference in interactive patterns of arguing is hard to explain in terms of the kind of people who marry or cohabit. But it fits well with the premise that the clarity of commitment and reduction in ambiguity when couples marry bring with them a whole load of security.

***

We first came up with the idea of STOP signs because I wanted a simple way of explaining the four bad habits that destroy relationships. Over the years, I've taught this idea to thousands of couples and new parents. You can read about it in more detail in my book *Let's Stick Together – The Relationship Book for New Parents.*[8]

By being honest about my own shortcomings, I found that most people could immediately spot their own STOP signs. My particular weaknesses were Opting out and Thinking the worst. Even as my marriage to Kate pulled out of its terrible nosedive and began to resemble something far more happy and normal, I knew I had an unfortunate tendency to assume I was in trouble with Kate unless shown otherwise.

When I was teaching this idea to a group of exhausted new mothers in a post-natal clinic, it would come across as funny. Most of them could relate to it. Alas, at home it was little short of a plague on our marriage.

As a simple example, Kate might point to the overflowing rubbish bin in the kitchen and say, "The bin is full." As we had six children, it was essential for us to share responsibilities. With so many things that needed doing, we had to work together as a team. Most of the time, we were good at it. Since Kate had her hands full with other things, it was a straightforward request for me to empty the bin.

Instead, what I heard was, "Harry, what were you thinking? Why haven't you emptied the bin yet? Now I'm cross with you. You're in trouble." Feeling under pressure, I would react in one of two ways. I would first empty the bin. But then either I'd find an excuse to head off to my office and hide, or I'd close down and stop talking. This was me Opting out.

This kind of reaction could happen at any time. I knew it was ridiculous. I was aware of it. I taught about it regularly. And yet the voice in my head that said, "You're in trouble, Harry" never left.

It was especially frustrating for Kate.

***

Tell me about it!

Before I launch into this, I need to put what I'm about to say into perspective. After the difficult early years of our marriage, life with Harry was unrecognizably better. Managing our growing family together meant that we had to be a good team, and we were. We were a great team. We were friends. We did things together. We talked about stuff. I felt he was on my side rather than just another part of my care package.

However, there was something missing. Our marriage was functional, like a well-baked cake, with a solid focus on the children and our secure friendship. It was a perfectly nice cake that did its job. But it cried out for a layer of icing that would transform it into something utterly delicious and special. The icing was a big dose of tenderness and kindness.

Harry was very much a man who did things in his own time. Many people would have said he was a wonderful father and husband, who was deeply involved in our family life. And he was, for much of the time.

But whenever I needed something specific to be done and asked him in the "wrong way", Harry would close down. Although he sometimes tried to explain, I never really understood what he meant by the "wrong way", or what the "right way" might be.

We mentioned "passivity" earlier. Well, this is what it looks like! It's only in recent years that we've figured out that this is what it is. It's the opposite of attentiveness, and therefore also the opposite of gentleness and kindness.

The most obvious examples of his passivity were when I needed something to happen. I often found it impossible to get his attention. Asking him directly sometimes worked: "Please will you do this." I had no idea why sometimes it worked and sometimes it didn't. Asking indirectly rarely worked. Being cross certainly didn't.

In recent years, Harry has worked from home. While he was upstairs in his office, I would be down in the kitchen taking responsibility for children and food. "Supper's ready," I would shout from the bottom of the stairs, expecting him to stop what he was doing and come down. No response. Because Harry didn't like shouting in our house, he didn't come immediately. He took his time. I knew this. But it was still incredibly frustrating. With a million things on my mind, it was so much easier to call upstairs. What was the problem with that?

The same thing would happen when I asked him to do something that I would otherwise have to do. "The bin's overflowing," I would say, before getting on with other things. It was thoroughly irritating to find it still overflowing a few hours later. Why couldn't he just empty it when I asked? It was as if he had blanked me.

To some extent, I was my own worst enemy. Harry had his own share of a million things on his mind. I suppose I could perfectly well have gone and found him upstairs in his office. I could have emptied the bin myself, or picked up the clothes myself, or finished the washing up myself. But so could he.

It wasn't ever a point-scoring or a fairness thing. It was simply an opportunity for him to respond to me with kindness and care. But because I said it wrongly, he closed down.

All of this jumping through hoops and playing mental word games was slowly driving me mad, mainly because I never understood how I was supposed to say things in the right way. Over the years, it closed me down, so that I stopped telling Harry about important things in my life and I stopped asking him things. I didn't think he was interested. Anyway, I felt tongue-tied.

I was "Opting out", and he never knew.

***

During my courses on relationships for new parents, I used to joke about how my default position in life was that "I was in trouble unless it was proved otherwise". This was because of my long-standing toxic combination of "Thinking the worst" and "Opting out".

It was bad enough during everyday life, hearing Kate point out something that needed doing as if she were telling me off. Being shouted at to come down for dinner sounded like a telling off. Being told that the bin was overflowing sounded like a telling off.

I only found out about the idea of passivity in recent years. But this is where my passivity came in. Doing things in my own time meant that I could stay in control. I may be in trouble but I can still be independent, my own boss.

Even if Kate's requests were invariably polite and reasonable, all I could hear was a voice from the past: "You're being shouted at"; "You haven't emptied the bin"; "You're in trouble".

I knew it wasn't real. It drove me mad too.

The run-up to our daughter's wedding multiplied this by a million. There'd been so much to organize in a short space of time, so many opportunities for Kate to ask me to do something. The result was that I spent much of the time feeling utterly closed. It wasn't healthy or positive. It put a big dent in my relationship with Kate.

Of course the wedding itself brought this time of prickliness to an end. It was a truly magical day for all the family. But it also strengthened my own resolve to deal with my natural inclination to "Think the worst" and "Opt out" once and for all.

A few weeks afterwards, we were relaxing on our summer holiday and I brought the subject up with Kate. Even if her muffled sigh told me the extent of her frustration and resignation, there was love in her eyes as she turned to me.

"But, Harry," she said, "you know I love you and want to be close to you."

I did. I really did know this. Kate had often told me how all she ever wanted was to be close to me.

For me, it was one of those light-bulb moments. I knew that this was the voice I needed to hear every time she looked at me, every time she shouted at me, every time she asked me to do something, every time she said anything at all.

It wasn't the way she said it that needed to change; it was the way I saw her. It was the voice I heard. It was the big picture. Kate wasn't out to get me. I wasn't in trouble. I had a wife who loved me and wanted to be close to me.

It was as simple as that.

***

Over the years, I'd become pretty cynical about Harry's new marriage wisdom. I loved him deeply and knew I was married to a good man whom I could trust. But I'd had it up to the eyeballs with yet another new method he'd read about from the research that promised to get the best out of our relationship.

After this conversation – "Beachgate", as we now call it! – I didn't expect any change. Yet, just as it had years ago after he'd read my job-spec letter, something clicked in his head.

All I know is that when Harry is kind and attentive, when he's interested and helpful, it's wonderful. A lot of kindness started happening. The result was that I no longer had to be frightened about the way I spoke to him. I no longer had to tread on eggshells. I could be free to be myself. Almost for the first time, I could be free to talk. I felt real softness, cherishing, and delight in the way Harry now treated me. Our friendship blossomed.

In the past, I'd probably not been very gentle with him because I'd been so muddled. I was always on the back foot: "Please do me a favour and hold the baby while I do the school run." It felt defensive. I'd never really felt equal. I even used to train the children how to speak to Daddy!

This was my problem, of course. But it was the way I responded to him. Now, all of a sudden, it seemed that he really enjoyed my company. He liked hanging out with me.

The funny thing is that my own "Thinking the worst" has gone away. Over the years, I'd never really accepted that he was proud of me when he said it. I never believed it because he wasn't attentive. Even when I was head cookery teacher at a cookery school and was often told how well I did, I could never really take it in.

The extraordinary thing is the extent to which I have grown in confidence because of the way my husband treats me. I have felt cherished. And I have responded in the way that a badly parched flower responds to desperately needed water. I can now hear his pride.

It's important to acknowledge here that a lot of this is my stuff. But it is in knowing that my husband is my friend, is attentive, is interested, and no longer reacts defensively as if he is in trouble, that I feel as if I have been set free.

He has changed his mindset. I have responded.

The result is that the last two years of our marriage have been the best ever.

Now when things go wrong and Harry is grumpy – and it obviously still does happen – I attribute it to something else and not to him. I know I am loved and adored. So I can handle anything.

***

Almost as if to remind us not to get complacent, even while we were writing this book we had an unfortunate example of how arguments and misunderstandings can sometimes appear out of the blue.

We had just finished running a marriage day for couples in our local community. The day had gone well, and Kate and I were feeling close and altogether pretty good about life.

The very next morning was the birthday of one of our children. It was also a Sunday, so we had plenty of time to get through our usual birthday traditions. These include the whole family sitting on our bed while the birthday girl or boy opens their goodies. There's always a lot of singing and wry comments about the quality of our early morning breath, and then we assemble in the kitchen for pancakes. The birthday child wears a special hat and sits on a special chair, both garishly decorated the previous day. So there's quite a lot to do.

After our late breakfast, the plan was to go for a family walk in the countryside and then come home and cook a late lunch or early dinner.

Because we live on a farm, there is also a whole cycle of animal feeding to be done every day. The morning round of lambs, chickens, horses, ducks, and dogs takes a good forty-five minutes. So I went off to do that, having made everyone aware that the weather forecast was for heavy rain from lunchtime. If we were to get our walk in before it rained, we would have to get on with it.

When I got back, the rest of the family had not got on with it. Everyone seemed far more relaxed than I was. Having started the day late, I became increasingly frustrated that events were beginning to run away from me. I still needed to finalize a talk I was due to give at a conference the following day.

I couldn't verbalize it but I was beginning to feel more and more out of control. I snapped at one of my family who was staying with us. I snapped at Kate. I snapped at the children.

What I needed at that moment was to be told that everything was OK, that it didn't matter if we left late, and nobody would mind getting wet on the walk. I could relax and take the day as it came.

Instead, I kept trying to steer the family onwards through the day, constantly on the back foot. I was trying to speed things up; Kate was trying to slow things down. I knew she was cross with me but, whatever I did, I felt I could do no right.

***

Since childhood, I've always been something of a people-pleaser. I need things to go right and I hate conflict of any kind.

Whenever Harry has got into a stew about anything, my first concern is that his behaviour might upset those around him. My feeling of worry about this can become incredibly strong, to the extent that I can get myself into a panic inside.

Normally, if Harry is under pressure at home, I will move

him away from the children and take over. He does the same for me. But, when we have friends or family around us, my absolute priority is to smooth the situation.

On this particular day, all I could see was Harry barking orders at us. I thought his behaviour was terrible. Our daughter came to me later in the day and asked if Dad was going to ruin her entire day. The final straw was when I asked him if everything was OK. He thrust his fingers out towards me and barked, "Don't."

***

I knew I'd blown it. I had to go to speak at the conference the following day. But as soon as I got back home I apologized to my daughter, who was typically forgiving. I also wanted to make it up to Kate. So I made sure to ask her often how she was, offer more than the usual cups of tea, and sort out dinners so that she wouldn't have to.

Throughout the week, Kate and I remained emotionally distant from one another. I knew we needed to make up before spending a weekend away with friends. Just before we arrived, I turned to Kate and asked if we were friends.

"Are we?" she asked. My attempt to break the ice wasn't working.

"Well, let's talk before we go in," I said.

"No," she said. "We're here and you've had the whole week." Whereupon the car rolled to a halt and Kate got out.

I felt completely crushed. My attempt to reach out had been rebuffed. I could barely move from my seat. The idea of facing friends with a smile on my face that I didn't feel inside was impossible.

***

I was livid. He'd had the whole week to apologize, and had waited until the last minute to try to make amends. I was not going to let more friends down.

By a miracle, our friends had left a note saying they had popped out for some shopping. I came back to the car to find an immobile and disconsolate Harry. I told him nobody was in and so he should come inside and talk.

Over the next half-hour, the ice thawed. He made no attempt to excuse his behaviour days earlier but simply threw up his hands to say sorry, he had failed to explain the pressure he had felt, and he had failed to apologize to me. "I just needed forgiveness. All I needed was a hug," he said.

Suddenly I realized how badly hurt he was. Throughout the week, I had been treating him as I would one of our children when they threw a tantrum in a supermarket. Instead of reacting to the tantrum, I had spent all week ignoring it and continuing with life in the hope that he would sort out his own stuff. My getting out of the car looked to him as if I had now reached the check-out desk and was about to abandon him altogether. I wouldn't and hadn't.

But my walk-away strategy was only partly right. Yes, on the day, Harry had thrown a tantrum and needed to sort himself out. But, through the rest of the week, what he had needed most was for me to go back and give him a hug. He was no longer a man behaving badly but a little boy in need of reassurance.

It may be up to the husband to take responsibility for the relationship. It may be the case that when husbands love their wives, the wives will love them right back. But sometimes a wife needs to acknowledge that even the best of husbands have their off days. Harry's off day turned into my off week.

Every now and then, a wife needs to take responsibility when her husband can't.

At risk of getting too deep and meaningful about all this, we can usually find the roots of our particular bad habits laid down and buried somewhere in our past. We react badly towards our loved ones because of the way we were treated, the messages we were given, the way we see ourselves, the things we most need.

Our own story is a salutary lesson on how the effects of parenting – both good and bad – can be very long-lasting indeed. The way each of us was brought up as a child took us on into adulthood with certain messages in our minds.

Some of those messages have proved really positive and helped us as a functional couple: You are independent. You have freedom to choose. You can do whatever you want to do. You will always be OK.

Other messages have been negative and led to dysfunction: You're in trouble. You're always putting pressure on us. You're tricky.

It's really important that this is not used as an excuse to blame or criticize our parents. After all, just as few of us wake up in the morning with the intention of being horrible to one another, it's highly unlikely that any of our parents set out to be anything less than the best they could be in the circumstances.

In an earlier chapter, we discussed how the worst kinds of divorce are those where the parents weren't fighting.[9] In a low-conflict split, parents are convinced they are doing what they think is best for themselves. The trouble is that their children will see things from a completely different perspective.

This can be true even in intact families. There's often a giant mismatch between what parents do and how their children receive it. All sorts of factors can then combine to make us as children take things in a certain way that our parents never intended.

For example, our parents love us in their own way, but we don't feel loved in the way we need. Our parents have high hopes for us, but we lack confidence in ourselves. Our parents are proud of us, but we now crave affirmation because they never showed it.

This applies as much to us as parents as to anyone else. However well we hope and plan to bring up our children, we are bound to blow it from time to time, and they are bound to take things the wrong way. We've often joked with our own children that we will pay for their counselling as adults! And we will, if that's what they want.

You've read how we finally dealt with the biggest bugbear that has held our marriage back for years. It was a voice from the past with a negative message that should never have applied to us. In fact, we were a fairly classic "Back off or Fire back" couple whose bad habits played on each other. It was only when we found the positive message to overwrite the old negative ones that we finally nailed the problem.

Talk to your spouse about the negative messages that hold you back: "*You'll never be good enough*"; "*You're only loved if you perform*"; "*You disappoint me*". These are the dysfunctional messages from your childhood, from school, from parents, from past relationships.

Now talk about what your spouse really thinks of you: "*I'm so proud of you*"; "*I love you*"; "*You deserve the best*"; "*You don't have to prove anything to me*"; "*There's nothing you can do to stop me loving you*".

We brought our messages to the surface by talking about them, by being friends. The lie was that Harry was always in trouble and that Kate could never believe what Harry said about her. The truth is that Kate loves Harry and wants to be close and that Harry is genuinely and justifiably proud of Kate.

Nobody says figuring out our deep messages will be easy. After all, it took us twenty-eight years, which is why our twenty-ninth and thirtieth years of marriage have been our best ever.

So far.

Back from the brink

Harry and Kate aren't the only couple who have peered into the marital abyss and stepped back. Their marriage today is unrecognizable from what went before. We tell three more stories of marriages that could so easily have ended. Instead, each has worked it out and gone on to be better than ever. We outline a route map for recovery.

Being married can be hard work.

Recently, we had the pleasure of meeting a lovely couple called Bill and Sylvia, who had just celebrated their sixty-eighth wedding anniversary.

"So what is your secret?" we asked them.

"You've got to work at your marriage," said Bill. "Keep it alive. Remember the woman you married."

"And you, Sylvia," we asked, "what do you think?"

"Everyone has difficult moments. So argue and get on with it," she replied with a big smile. Then she stopped and thought for a moment. "Mind you, sometimes I could have throttled him!"

They're not the only couple to have gone through their fair share of ups and downs. As we've said several times already, there's a reason why we say "for better, for worse" in our wedding vows.

Our survey of 291 mothers found that half of today's "happy" couples said they had been "unhappy" at some stage and a quarter had been "very unhappy".[1]

Unhappiness is not the end of the relationship. But nor is it a permanent state.

Of those who said they had been "unhappy" and had stuck it out, three-quarters were now "happy" in their marriage. Among those who had been "very unhappy" and stuck it out, over half were now "happy" and one in five "very happy".

So it's not only couples like Bill and Sylvia who have had their bad moments. It's a normal phenomenon.

Nor is it only couples like Harry and Kate, who have stood precariously on the brink of divorce and turned back to improve their marriage for the better. Others have been there and come back with better, stronger marriages.

Here are a few of the real-life couples that we know personally, all of whom have come "back from the brink", or at the very least have survived testing circumstances and come through stronger. Like ours, each marriage remains a work in progress.

As with our other stories, we have changed their names and camouflaged their details.

***

Brian and Paula's story flits between comedy and tragedy. Some of their story is utterly awful and it's easy to sympathize with the difficulties they have had to face. Other parts are sufficiently funny that it's hard not to laugh out loud. But theirs is a good example of a couple who toughed out what many consider the most difficult phase of marriage – the early years of parenthood – and now have a solid marriage rooted in friendship and kindness.

Their relationship began, and nearly ended, in the workplace.

After finishing university, Brian and Paula met as fellow management trainees on a graduate scheme with an office supplies company based just outside London. They fell in love almost immediately and were married within eighteen months of their first kiss.

Each of them entered marriage with a traditional view of the world. Both had been brought up in strong families where marriage for life was the norm. Marriage was a given. Divorce wasn't an option.

This was only ever a positive expectation. "Happy ever after" was the dream for both of them. In Paula's case, it was all she had hoped for for as long as she could remember. Brian played the part of romantic suitor and swept her off her feet. Their friendship grew.

Six months into the marriage, Paula discovered she was pregnant. At almost the same time, Brian was offered a new post in a regional office. Their employers didn't appear to take into account that this would pose a big problem for the newly-weds, with Paula still working in the headquarters office near London. It was a take-it-or-leave-it kind of offer.

Paula's request for a similar move fell on deaf ears. They said they needed her too much where she was. Since Paula was going to have to stop work sooner or later anyway, she and Brian decided to accept his new job offer and move away. Reluctantly, she handed in her notice.

Moving to an unfamiliar city meant they left behind their families and friends. They also now had to cope as an expanding family on one salary. By the time their first child was born, the differences between them were beginning to show up as cracks in their relationship.

Paula liked to be fastidiously tidy at home. Everything had a place where it needed to stay when not being used. In contrast, Brian was more free-spirited, liberally distributing himself and his belongings around the flat, possibly assuming either that some tidy-fairy would magically put stuff away, or that it didn't matter anyway. Alas, it mattered like mad to Paula, who became increasingly frustrated, thinking that he didn't care.

Brian's approach to food was similarly free-spirited. He loved to cook but he hated to wash up. This proved difficult for Paula as she was generally a lot less interested in food but also the one left at home to clear up Brian's experimental messes.

Paula was not a natural mother. After a complicated delivery, their new baby would not settle into a regular feeding or sleeping routine. Paula became deeply unsatisfied with parenthood in general. Although Brian was an involved father, his input was limited because of work pressures. Lacking nearby support from family and friends, Paula was permanently exhausted. Their situation became yet more complicated when Brian was made redundant within months of their move. Rather than return to London, they decided to stick it out while Brian started his own business.

Their relationship had just enough love and spark, as well as commitment to marriage, to see them through these tiring first few months as new parents. But these were not happy times. The combination of exhaustion and big differences between them made them bicker often. Not learning from their first experience, Paula quickly became pregnant with their second child, who also failed to settle into much of a sleep pattern.

The low moment for their marriage came one evening as Brian was working late with his new employees. Struggling to cope with a newborn suffering from croup – a horrible and distinctive-sounding cough that also causes breathing problems – and a two-year-old refusing to sleep, in desperation Paula abandoned the toddler at home and got into her car with the baby.

To the dismay of his embarrassed employees, Paula then marched into Brian's office and handed over the baby, saying, "Here. You're the father. *You* sort this out," before marching out and returning home.

Over the next few weeks, Paula and Brian established a new routine whereby they divided responsibility for the children between them. Brian became primary parent for the two-year-old and Paula took on the baby.

Their obvious difficulties descended into farce when they began to talk about separating. Having broached the subject, they found they couldn't split up because neither of them wanted to cope with the children on their own!

It was only by the grace of God, they now say, that neither of them had an affair. Had an opportunity presented itself at this low point, either of them could well have been tempted.

Realizing they needed to figure out a better way to make their marriage work, they persuaded their parents to look after the children for a weekend while they attended a marriage course.

The course helped them to understand a lot more about how to walk in each other's shoes, about what it is like being the other person. It also helped them realize how their isolation from family had made them vulnerable. They now surround themselves with supportive friends. Marriage is hard to do on your own.

Even through their difficulties, Paula had always known that Brian wanted the best for her. As a result of the course, he realized that his attempts to fix her problems with mild depression had not been helpful. Now he knows that he needs to sit and listen more often instead of coming up with quick-fix solutions. Paula also really appreciates how Brian shows her love in the way she wants it. He is very attentive and always aware of what is going on in her life.

Today, their children are now approaching their teens. As a couple, Brian and Paula are very aware of their shortcomings. They bicker and nag one another over the same differences they have always had with tidiness and money. But they also know beyond doubt that they love each other and have to keep working at their marriage. As much as possible they keep their focus on what is good in the marriage, rather than bad. And they have learned to be quick to forgive each other.

No marriage will ever be perfect, least of all theirs. But Brian and Paula have a big-picture view of their marriage as being for life. It is secure and content, if occasionally messy, and always worth it.

They describe their marriage as "real".

***

Paul and Jane are another young couple with two small children.

After they met at a party, their friendship developed slowly into a full-blown love affair, if anything encouraged more by Jane than by Paul.

Paul worked as a teacher in a primary school and had had one previous girlfriend. Jane was an administrator for her local church office. Paul was her first boyfriend.

Two years after they met, Paul had fallen for Jane every bit as much as she had for him. They got married and settled into what promised to be a happy life together.

Just as happened to us, the birth of their children exposed the underlying weakness in their relationship. Jane withdrew from work to become a mother, revelling in her new role. Although she was still besotted with Paul, the distraction of children left him feeling neglected.

Paul focused more and more of his energy on work as the couple drifted apart without even realizing it. Whenever their first child became ill, Jane took over anything child-related, whether feeding, bathing, changing, or dressing. In effect, Paul was sidelined as a father. It wasn't a conscious decision. Had it been pointed out to Jane, she would have defended it as only natural.

The result was that Paul focused ever more of his time and energy on work. Jane barely noticed the drift, consumed with the joys and challenges of motherhood as their second child was born.

Receiving little attention from Jane at home, Paul found it elsewhere. This was not in any way deliberate. It just kind of happened. Furtive glances exchanged with an attractive fellow teacher led to seemingly innocent conversations, initially about school and then moving on to home life. The pressure of catching up on paperwork and marking became excuses for staying on at school late.

The affair began.

Six months on and Jane had begun to notice that Paul seemed increasingly distant from her. "I don't feel love for you any more," he replied when she asked what was wrong. Jane's world exploded.

They came to see us largely at Jane's instigation. She was clearly distraught. Paul seemed indifferent. Initially, we spent three sessions with them. As we always do when we ask couples to tell their story, we asked if there was anything else they needed to talk about. Each of them said no. Paul didn't mention the affair. Nor did Jane have any idea.

For a while, things seemed to be improving between them. Jane appreciated Paul's renewed interest in her and their children. There were more conversations and less bickering. Then suddenly, out of the blue, Paul announced that he was moving out. He claimed he felt unable to cope with the pressure to change that seemed to fall disproportionately on his shoulders. Jane clung to the hope that Paul would eventually come to his senses. She kept her responses to the older child's questions about the whereabouts of Daddy deliberately vague.

A week away as a family in a rented cottage during the school holidays gave her hope that their marriage might be salvageable. Paul showed that he still cared about her. The day before their return home, Paul went out to the shops. Jane innocently picked up the phone that he had inadvertently left behind. The stream of lurid texts to another woman was much less of a shock than she might have expected.

Paul readily confessed to his affair when confronted by Jane on his return. He seemed profoundly apologetic and relieved. There was no acrimony. Paul said the affair would stop from that moment. He asked for Jane's forgiveness.

Paul moved back into the family home, though not into the marital bed. He responded willingly to Jane's need to revisit every conversation and action they had had during the previous year. Jane's remarkable willingness to forgive was made easier – if easier is the right word – by Paul's willingness to be open. They talked for hours at a time without any hint of bickering.

At the time of writing this book, Paul and Jane have survived a year since their reconciliation on that family holiday. Their marriage, all but over a year ago, is still very much intact, undoubtedly vulnerable, but also filled with real hope and rekindled love.

Few would criticize Jane for kicking Paul out of the house and filing for divorce. He broke their marriage vows in the same way that men and women have done since marriage began. He failed in his responsibility to his wife and fell for another woman.

But, better late than never, Paul has finally realized what an amazing woman he married.

Aside from talking to us and two other friends, Jane has never washed her dirty linen in public. Her family and neighbours know they had problems, but not the details. Her own determination to live up to the commitment she made when she got married gave her the patience and tolerance to face up to their problems and seek help, all the while keeping her focus on being the brilliant mother that she is.

From the moment Paul's foolishness was exposed, he has at last stepped up to the plate and taken responsibility for his marriage. His attitude is humble and gentle, even meek. Although Jane's questioning occasionally makes him feel defensive, he accepts that openness is his only course of action if he is to retain the wife he now knows he loves. He knows he needs to take the heat.

Two key factors have allowed Paul and Jane to come through this stronger than ever. The first is that Jane has had continuous support from her friends. She has never felt judged. They have never given her unwanted advice, nor have they expressed anger against Paul.

Instead, they have been there for both of them. They have sat with the children so that Paul and Jane can have time to themselves. And they have listened to Jane while she processed the whole experience. They've provided a sounding board that has allowed Jane to get through the anger and blame stages of grief far more quickly than might have been the case without support. It's also strengthened their friendship because they've seen Jane at her worst.

The second factor is that Jane's remarkable capacity for forgiveness has collided with Paul's renewed decision to be the man she originally married. Paul and Jane have encountered about the worst problem a marriage can possibly experience. The affair was never deliberate. It shows how a perfectly good relationship can go wrong. But it also shows how two good people can lean on the commitment they share to turn something bad into something wonderful.

At the moment, their back-from-the-brink recovery is very much a work in progress. It would be tempting to describe their relationship as fragile. But that's not quite right. They are secure but careful, in the same way that two explorers in an unfamiliar land would be alert to danger as they set out on a new adventure.

Ultimately, their story is a great advertisement for marriage.

***

To their friends, Jack and Emily seemed the perfect couple.

Like us, they got married on a beautiful English summer's day in June. Everything about their relationship seemed right. They looked great. They both had promising careers, Jack as an engineer in a consultancy firm, Emily as a corporate lawyer. They were even widely known as "the Perfects". People used to make disparaging jokes about how impossibly well matched they were, while secretly envying their good fortune in finding each other and living the dream of "happily ever after".

On their third anniversary, Jack announced to Emily in a matter-of-fact way that he was unsure whether he really wanted to be married to her. She was so shocked that she changed the subject immediately, refusing even to acknowledge it, lest it ruin their anniversary dinner.

Emily decided that denial was her best strategy for stopping it from ruining her life. To prevent the thought of Jack leaving from preying on her mind, she buried herself in work. At night, however, there was no escape. For months afterwards, she cried herself to sleep. Meanwhile, the state of their marriage went ignored and undiscussed. Life continued as if nothing had happened. They never spoke about it in private, and in public their friends had no idea.

As part of his professional development, Jack went off on a week's leadership course. When he returned, he told Emily that he had been thinking about their marriage and had decided to stay. He said it as if it were a fait accompli. That was it. It had been decided.

For the next few years, their marriage continued its shell-like existence, beautiful on the outside but empty within. Then Emily became pregnant. The birth of their daughter gave both parents a new sense of functional purpose but little in the way of romance or friendship. They were the opposite of many couples. They liked one another but didn't love one another.

The turning point came when Emily's father became very ill

with cancer. Emily had always been close to both her parents, even though she knew that their relationship had been rocky at times. Her father's subsequent death hit her very hard. At the funeral, she experienced a profound and unexpected deepening of her nominal Christian faith. It caused her to re-evaluate every aspect of her life, including her marriage.

Jack noticed her new softer and more open attitude towards him. Whereas before Emily had tended to keep her thoughts and feelings to herself, now she began talking to Jack about her hopes and fears. It showed Jack a side of Emily that he had not seen before. He loved hearing about her life. He suddenly realized that he really wanted to make his marriage work. For the first time, he knew he didn't want to lose her.

On the marriage course at their local church, both Jack and Emily learned that successful couples were open and unselfish towards one another. They also learned about the power of forgiveness.

Soon afterwards, Jack told Emily that he needed to talk to her that evening as he had something important to say. Emily was suddenly very frightened that he was going to tell her he had cancer. Instead, he admitted to a string of affairs that he had had during their fallow years before having children. He asked for her forgiveness. Emily burst into tears, nodding. She told him of her shame that she had had an affair during a business trip. She too needed forgiveness.

Jack and Emily are another amazing couple. They didn't start out that way. Both were unaware of quite how selfish they were. Their marriage was founded more on tradition than on love and commitment to the future. But they had gone with the flow. Jack wanted the outward appearance of marriage but not the commitment to one person. Emily's identity and security were tied more to her work than to her marriage. How they stayed married in spite of their mutual infidelity is a mystery.

Their rediscovery of one another was sparked by the tragic death of Emily's father. The renewal of their marriage bounced off Emily's decision to be more open and vulnerable and then some key lessons learned on a marriage course. But, ultimately, their marriage rests on openness and forgiveness. It was Jack who risked everything by admitting to his affairs, prompting Emily to make her own admission. That was the key step in securing their future together.

Without that admission, it seems highly unlikely that they could ever have reached the level of emotional intimacy that they now enjoy. Each of them would always have had a dark space in their marriage that could never be shared. Having strayed once, or more, there was also less of a barrier to doing it again.

Instead, their honesty and humility towards one another have given them the marriage that they never knew they craved. Today they are proud not to be perfect. Reminders of the past come up unexpectedly from time to time and threaten to sabotage them. They have to remember that they have forgiven each other. Talking about it and staying open to one another, no matter how tired or upset they might be, is what stops the bad old ways from returning.

Jack and Emily credit their turnaround to a miracle. Nonetheless, their renewed marriage is now firmly rooted in a new attitude, a new sense of meaning, and new support from friends in their faith community.

Wise friends

The best hope for a struggling marriage is a wise friend, ideally a wise couple. Wise friends listen well, don't take sides, want your marriage to succeed, and know what's normal, but can also confront. We have had various wise friends along the way who held us to account, sat us down, gave us a route map, and supported and encouraged us. One of the many reasons we never send couples for relationship counselling is that counsellors tend to view you as two individuals. Wise friends see the bigger picture and the longer view. Here's how you can be a wise friend to couples you know.

A friend of ours pops over for a glass of wine or a cup of tea.

"So, how are things at home?" we ask casually.

It's one of those open questions that usually get palmed off with the response "Fine, thanks." This quickly morphs into, "The kids are all well; Rob/Jill is away a lot," and, if we're lucky, "But I'm OK" – followed by a sigh.

We move on and talk about other things.

But how do we react when, instead of giving the standard response, our friend hesitates before answering? We know immediately that something is up. Their head drops and they reply softly.

"Not so good. Rob/Jill and I have started going to counselling." Or, "We are thinking about splitting up." Or, "I think he's/she's having an affair."

After we've got over the initial shock, do we have any idea what to do or say next that will help them, and that will be in their best interests?

Will we be wise friends?

***

Most struggling couples don't need therapy or counselling. They just need a bit of practical inspiration and hope.

It's especially striking that, in the year before couples split up, 60 per cent of married parents and 80 per cent of unmarried parents report that they are quite happy with their relationship and not arguing too much.[1] In effect, most break-ups come out of the blue. One moment couples are quite happy; the next they've split up.

Logically, it must be the case that many of these happy couples ought not to be splitting up at all. Their relationships are eminently salvageable. And although research in this area is difficult, just as it is with counselling, there is more than enough evidence to show that couples who do a marriage or relationship course tend to end up happier, with less conflict, and with improved odds of staying together.[2]

So the starting point for a wise friend is to recommend a course. It might be all they need.

In the UK, the most popular one is called The Marriage Course.[3] In the US and other countries, the best-known course is called PREP.[4] Other excellent courses – including Marriage Encounter,[5] PREPARE/ENRICH,[6] and FOCCUS[7] – can be found in many countries, courtesy of our friends at Google.

***

Apart from pointing couples towards a marriage course, what else can a wise friend do, and what does it take to be a wise friend? (We'll come back to the option of counselling later.)

Let us start by telling you about some of the friends who have helped us along the way. Then we'll try to distil what we think are the key characteristics of a wise friend: what characteristics to look out for in others or to develop in yourself.

None of what wise friends do is especially difficult. Three couples in particular helped us when our marriage got into trouble and as we started to rebuild something new and better.

Unlike in the rest of the book, where we've changed names, we're using their real names here in order to honour them as the wise friends they are.

The first person to pick up on our problems was a lovely lady called Ali. She definitely was, and is, a wise friend.

Ali and I had known each other for about five years. She'd given birth to twins at about the time we had our second daughter. We'd shared a lot of the stresses and joys of motherhood. Harry also got on very well with her husband, Steve.

Because we had such a strong relationship, I felt I could tell Ali that Harry and I had problems. I never felt judged by her and I never sensed that she took sides. She might acknowledge something unflattering I said about Harry, but she would never put him down. I wouldn't have wanted that anyway.

It felt safe talking to her because she took me seriously.

Eventually, I also told her about the other man I had started seeing. I knew that what I was doing was wrong. The "affair" hadn't yet got out of hand, but just talking about it with somebody was incredibly helpful. Getting it out in the open meant that it was no longer a secret. Telling a friend took away a lot of the power of the forbidden. The result was that it was easier to do the right thing.

Because she had spent so much time hearing my story, it also felt appropriate to get advice from her. When she heard about the other man, Ali was very clear and direct with me. She told me I had to end this fledgling relationship straight away.

But she didn't just leave me stranded in a bad marriage. She knew that cutting off something that had appeared to hold so much promise, in order to go back to my marriage with Harry (which didn't), would leave me in a state of grief. So she was the one who arranged for me to have our meeting with my vicar, John, and his wife, Corinne.

Although I didn't know John and Corinne nearly as well, I knew them enough to see that they were both lovely, no-nonsense people who oozed compassion and wisdom. Their position of authority – as vicar and wife – gave me the platform from which I could make it crystal clear to Harry what the problem was. They provided a safe setting for us and managed that first crucial meeting where we finally began to deal with our marriage problem.

They reinforced the message I had heard from Ali that my fledgling extra-marital relationship had to stop. I didn't feel at all judged by them because of the gentle way they told me. They also added to a growing list of voices telling me that my unhappiness was neither unique nor hopeless. Harry was not the only English bloke who was emotionally closed. I was not alone, and there were ways through these things.

It's not so much that they gave me a glimmer of hope – because I wasn't yet ready to believe it – but that they stopped me from descending into full-blown despair.

Ali and Steve then arranged our dinner a few nights later. After *hearing Harry's extraordinary comment that what he liked about me was the way I understood the chemistry of cooking, it was they who encouraged Harry to get started with some one-to-one counselling and recommended a place for him to go.*

***

Without the love and help of these wise friends, I am certain that our marriage would have continued its downward drift and eventually come to a confused end that neither of us wanted.

During those first few days and weeks when I was made aware of the problem, I never felt judged. Even though I could acknowledge what they were telling me – that I needed to make some changes pretty quickly even if I had no idea what they might be – I had confidence in our friends. They were just there.

I'd known Steve and Ali for several years and liked them a lot. So when they suggested I go off to counselling, I trusted them. They even helped me organize it.

For months afterwards, they were always on the end of a phone or available for coffee or a meal. I had some great one-to-one chats with Steve about being a husband and a father. It may have taken me six months to make that mental shift towards making Kate my number-one priority but, in my mind, those conversations with Steve were undoubtedly helpful and moved me in the right direction.

At no stage did he or Ali ever make me feel foolish or belittle me. Nor were they ever disparaging towards Kate. Nor did anyone tell me my marriage to Kate was over. I always felt they were on our side.

Looking back, it was probably more important that Kate got more of the support from our wise friends at the beginning. She was the one who was most aware of our shortcomings and she was most in need of somebody to hold her hand along the way.

What I needed at the start was encouragement to hang on in there and the occasional practical pointer to tell me what to do next.

From my point of view, Ali and Steve were the key friends at this most vulnerable stage, whereas John and Corinne were more in the background. But, because I trusted them so much, later on I was able to call on Corinne for advice about a particular relationship problem in my workplace. Her wise words helped me to see a new way of dealing with the matter, which was quickly resolved.

There were other amazing couples who were there along the way, quietly supporting our marriage, never taking sides. David and Lou, David and Ruth, Len and Jill, Greg and Cathy, Kurt and Hilary, Nicky and Sila are some of the names we honour – and, if any of you read this, thank you!

One other couple stand out for us. They came into our lives a few years on from our crisis point. We met Arthur and Jenny through the marriage courses that we ran for a while in the UK. They are a few years older and, like us, have a big family. As well as helping us with the odd marital dispute – which we wrote about earlier in chapter eight – I especially remember one moment years ago when the four of us were sitting together in our kitchen.

We were talking about how marriage requires so much work. Arthur turned to me and said this.

"Harry, you know, after thirty-eight years together, our marriage has become almost effortless."

As I asked him to clarify what he meant, he talked about the years of good habits that he and Jenny had built into their marriage – such as the deliberate choice to spend particular times of day together or the way they dealt with the inevitable little squabbles that crop up in most marriages. After so many years, he now didn't even have to think about doing this. It just happened.

I was both stunned and thrilled. If you do something enough, it should become automatic. But I had never heard anybody apply this idea to marriage. This seemed like confirmation.

Even if what Arthur said didn't necessarily guarantee that our own marriage would become similarly "effortless", it highlighted the likelihood of a pay-off for all the effort we were putting in now.

It feels, at long last, as if we are reaping that reward now.

We are not the only ones these wise friends have helped along the way. They have helped many others, just as we try to do ourselves. Some of what we all do is formal. Much of it is informal.

We have distilled what we think are some sensible principles to apply if you want to be wise friends to other couples, or find wise friends for yourself. It's probably easier to start with how to spot a foolish friend.

A foolish friend will:

- **Take sides.** "He didn't deserve you. I never thought he was good for you."

- **Downplay the marriage.** "If it's not working, you must do what's right for you. After all, it's your happiness that counts."

- **Jump to conclusions.** "That proves she doesn't care."

- **Give advice too quickly.** "Kick him out and change the locks. That's what I'd do."

- **Encourage separation or divorce.** "Follow your heart. You only have one life."

In contrast, a wise friend will:

- **Notice a red flag.** "You hinted that things aren't good at home. Let's go for a coffee."

- **Establish and maintain a rapport.** "How are you guys doing? Let's keep talking."

- **Take you seriously.** "This is important. Don't brush it under the carpet."

- **Take your marriage seriously.** "We won't take sides. It's your marriage that counts."

- **Create opportunities to talk.** "Come round for dinner. Both of you."

- **Be quick to listen and slow to speak.** "I see ... Uh huh ... Goodness ... And then?"

- **Take time.** "We don't have to sort this all out now. Let's work out what needs doing first."

- **Normalize**. "We found that having young children was the hardest phase of our married life. A lot of people say that. You're in a phase. It's difficult, but it will get a lot easier."

- **Share appropriately.** "Something similar happened to us a few years ago."

- **Know your limitations.** "Have you ever considered the possibility that you might be depressed? Have you thought about talking to your doctor about this?"

If you want to be a wise friend, there are two basic scenarios.

Scenario one is where you notice a couple who appear not to be getting on well – maybe they're neighbours or friends – but they haven't talked to you about it yet.

Scenario two is where somebody, whether an individual on their own or a couple together, comes to you and tells you their marriage is in trouble.

Let's start with **scenario one**, the easy one: the couple you notice who seem to be having problems.

To intervene or not to intervene... Of course you should, but not in the way you might think. And you certainly shouldn't go piling in with a whole bunch of unsolicited advice. A wise man called Selwyn Hughes once talked about building the bridge of empathy long before you try to drive the truck of confrontation across it. And, even after you've built the bridge, it might be the case that you should just leave it at that.

Tea, food, walks, and listening are the ways to build empathy.

Invite your friends or neighbours for a cup of tea and ask them how they are doing. You can say what you've noticed, but be tentative about it. You might have got the wrong end of the stick, in which case you will be embarrassed. Your role is then to give them an opportunity to speak if they wish and not if they don't. You have opened your door to them; it's up to them whether they choose to open up their life to you. And, if they don't, it's no longer your job to pry.

Our friend Ali is actually a highly skilled therapist in her day job. But her contribution as a wise friend, when our marriage was in the doldrums, was almost entirely to listen. Listening gave Kate a chance to get it all off her chest.

Ali took Kate seriously. She gave her time. She didn't offer unsolicited advice or take sides. She didn't rubber-stamp our separation, or put Harry down. She built the bridge of empathy long before suggesting a meeting with John and Corinne. When we sat down for a meal with her and her husband, Steve, they asked questions afterwards before suggesting counselling. Neither of them gave advice. Between them, they made two suggestions, both of which we acted on. What preceded their suggestions, especially the first, was a great deal of listening.

Ali now asks friends if they'd like to come with her while she walks her dog. The two big advantages of a dog walk are that it may be less threatening than a chat over coffee or tea. It's a bit like the best way to talk to a teenager. With no eye contact and an exit route at the end of the walk, there's less need to be defensive, to justify yourself.

It must have been tempting at times for them to give advice. After all, these are two of the wisest friends we know. Yet they used their wisdom by listening.

In order to have the right to speak, you first need to listen.

***

Now let's think about **scenario two**, the couple who come to see you.

Opinions differ on whether it's better to sit down with one person or both. Personally, we will take whatever we can get. But we prefer both spouses to come along. Sorting out a marriage alone is quite possible: if one person changes for the better, the other is likely to do so too. It's not easy, but it's possible. The odds are a great deal better if both spouses are in on the same plan. It's also a lot easier to see what's really going on when the couple are sitting next to you, rather than having to rely on one side of the story.

Once again, give them enough time and space to talk. We usually start by asking each person to tell the other their interpretation of how they got here, starting from when they first met. While each person speaks, the other should listen quietly without interrupting. We are very directive if they try to interrupt or disagree.

"Wait, let him talk. Please just listen. You'll have a chance to put your view across in a moment."

While they are telling their stories, we are watching and listening.

The first thing we're looking for is **evidence of commitment**. Did both of them fully buy into the relationship at the beginning? It's astonishing how many times we find that the man – and it's usually the man – was not totally convinced. Making a decision, buying in, profoundly affects men's commitment, far more than is the case for women.

In chapter six, we told you the story of Peter and Elena. It was only when they came to see us and Peter told his story that Elena found out for the first time how he had felt pressured into marriage. He had never really bought in. She was deeply shocked.

An imbalance in commitment matters because power in a relationship rests with the person who is less committed. That person is then less worried about pulling the plug if things go wrong. This is one of the best explanations for why cohabiting couples are so much more likely to fall into the pattern of behaviour that we called "Back off or Fire back" in chapter nine. One partner is uninterested or ambivalent. The other ends up treading on eggshells to preserve the status quo.

The next thing we're looking for is **the way two individuals talk about their marriage**. A couple came to see us fairly recently on the recommendation of other wise friends. It seemed like a last-ditch effort, but our friends thought each of them would relate to our story.

As each of them recounted their respective story of how they got to where they were now, a big difference emerged in terms of the language they used. Whereas the wife talked about "our marriage" and "our future" and "We did this" and "We do that", the husband talked about how "I have changed" or "I have really worked at it". His language was focused entirely on himself, not his wife. This may not be wilfully selfish, but it suggested that his priority was not the well-being of his wife or the success of their marriage. He was focused on himself.

Then we're looking for **patterns between them**. This means positive ones as well as negative. After all, it's good to be able to encourage a couple.

"It was really lovely watching you listen to his story."

"I liked the way you reached out to her arm. It was a moment of tenderness."

Eye contact is the most obvious pattern to look for. It shows interest. A person who makes little or no eye contact is either not interested or not paying attention. They might be thinking what to say next, but they're unlikely to be hearing what's being said. Smile as you point it out.

"Forgive me for saying so, but it's really hard to listen if you don't listen with your eyes. Could you do that?"

Negative patterns are all too easy to spot. Whenever an element of stress or pressure enters the conversation, somebody often reveals their STOP signs. One of them responds by making some tit-for-tat comment – Scoring points. Something gets misinterpreted that is clearly not what was meant – Thinking the worst. One of them looks away and physically switches off – Opting out. Eyes are rolled or some comment slips out that is dismissive at best and contemptuous at worst – Putting down. It's easiest to point it out by referring to our own STOP signs.

"I noticed you closing down when he was talking to you. I sometimes do that when I feel under pressure. The trouble is that it sends the terrible message that I don't care. I don't mean to do that. What message do you think it sends to him?"

Positive patterns are usually most apparent by their absence. It's obvious that the couple don't spend time with one another, do stuff together, sit down and talk, hug or hold hands, bring some little present home that shows they are being thoughtful. This is where the five Love Languages – Time, Words, Actions, Gifts, and Touch – can be so useful. They're easy to explain and easy to understand.

"Let's just stop for a second. I want to tell you about an idea called Love Languages, which helps explain how we can give love in our own way but not feel loved."

Look for opportunities to **tell a bit of your own story**. So much of the time, couples feel alone. By telling your story, you're making them feel normal. Misunderstandings, hurts, and difficulties are all pretty normal in a healthy relationship – because we all get it wrong it from time to time. That's why we've put so much of our own story into this book. There's bound to be something of our experience to which almost everybody can relate.

"We went through something quite similar a few years ago. It took us ages to deal with it, but we're much better at it now. Here's what happened... "

And, finally, we always make sure we ask **if there's anything else**. If one of these hasn't come up already, we're looking for evidence of the four "A"s: **Abuse, Addiction, Adultery, Abandonment**. All are grave abuses of trust in a relationship. Marriages *can* recover from these. But it's really hard. Couples don't always tell us. One time when we asked if there was anyone else involved, the husband lied straight to our faces. We only found out six months later, shortly after his wife did. When we mentioned this, he said he remembered and had felt guilty about lying. He apologized profusely. If people don't want to tell us, that's up to them. We can only ask.

"Is there anything else that's going on?"

Even if we've been talking things through in an informal way over a cup of coffee or perhaps while walking the dog, it's worth trying to finish the conversation by reminding them of the one thing they are going to do next. It could be a simple piece of homework or something they are going to do for one another. It might be an agreement for each of them to watch out for their particular worst STOP sign. It might be a plan to phone or text one another once a day at work to find out how each other's day is going. It might be a recognition that the husband needs to buy into the relationship properly. It might be that the couple need to forgive one another. It might be an agreement to have another chat in a week's time. It might be an agreement to read this book or *Let's Stick Together*, or to consider signing up for a marriage course.

Marriage is everybody's business. When somebody talks about their marriage, take it seriously.

***

A note on couple counselling
Many people feel helpless when faced with a friend whose marriage is on the rocks. So the obvious thing to do is to encourage them to sit down with somebody who does know what they are doing.

"Have you tried marriage guidance or relationship counselling?" seems like a sensible route. And so it can be.

Counselling can make a difference. But its success rates are much lower than we might hope or expect.

Much as we described earlier with marriage courses, research into the effectiveness of counselling is difficult to conduct. The ideal study would take a group of couples with similar marital problems, tell half of them they will receive counselling and half that they won't, and see what happens. This is called a randomized control trial. Alas, gold-standard studies like this remain thin on the ground because counselling organizations hate the idea of refusing treatment to anybody. Their assumption is that counselling works. But, unless studies run this kind of experiment, it's hard for counsellors or anyone else to be sure one way or the other.

Not surprisingly, the studies that do exist involve fairly small numbers. The best of them tend to suggest that counselling is beneficial for a little over half of couples. Within two years, half of these couples have reverted to their old problems or split up. This suggests a medium-term success rate of around one-third.[8]

That might not seem too bad. By way of comparison, this is similar to the fairly low odds that the average unmarried parents will stay together while bringing up their children, but a long way short of the much higher odds that the average married parents will stay together.[9]

You might think that if counselling were as effective as is sometimes claimed, couples ought to be able to do a bit better than the average unmarried parents.

Where there is clarity, of sorts, is in the widespread agreement among researchers that different methods of counselling tend to produce similar outcomes. In other words, it doesn't seem to matter what type of counselling you get. All have much the same effect.

Here's a throwaway comment in the introduction to a 2006 paper in the *Journal of Family Therapy*:[10]

In these comparisons, it's not been possible to verify measurable differences between therapy approaches.

Professor John Gottman, in the 1998 *Annual Review of Psychology*, is more striking:[11]

… it does not seem to matter very much what one does in treatment. In general the effect sizes are roughly the same, regardless of the exact nature of the intervention… almost all marital treatment effects to date would be due to non-specifics such as trust in the therapist, hope, the existence of

a structured program, all of which could be considered to be placebo effects.

This is a pretty astonishing statement. Here is one of America's best-known and most respected experts on marriage research concluding from the evidence that counselling or therapy per se isn't what helps couples. It's the fact of sitting down with somebody who cares, shows interest in you and your story, and has some sort of plan.

Let's make it clear that there are some really good counsellors out there. But there are also some shockers.

In the last chapter, we introduced you to Paul and Jane, the couple with young children who are now doing so well. What we didn't tell you was that, a couple of weeks before they came to see us, they had been to see a relationship counsellor with a respected organization.

Paul had started by telling the counsellor he had fallen out of love with his wife. Jane then talked about how distraught she was. The counsellor encouraged them to talk about it, whereupon they started bickering.

After a while the counsellor stopped them, before announcing with shocking clarity, "I can see what you mean. You two are completely incompatible. You would be better off apart."

Despite the difficulty of their situation – at this stage, Paul hadn't admitted to the affair he was still having – Paul and Jane were both equally taken aback by this suggestion. They had come for help with their marriage. Telling them to split up was an outrageous suggestion.

They didn't go back.

We'd like to think that our own input helped Paul and Jane put their marriage back together again. But, in the immediate aftermath of finding out about the affair, it was the support of wise friends that made it possible for Jane to forgive Paul.

"I don't think I could have done it without my friends," she told us. "Nobody tried to tell me what to do. Nobody had a go at Paul. And the only time I got really angry in front of a friend, she challenged me about my anger. I think if I'd tried to get through this on my own, I would have ended up very ill. It would have consumed me, and the outcome would have been very different."

***

If you're planning to see a counsellor yourself, or thinking about encouraging a friend to go, there are three reasonable questions you could ask to which you need sensible answers:[12]

- Will you help me save my marriage?

- Will you tell me how?

- What is your track record?

Many counsellors will baulk at these questions:

- "I help individuals, people, not marriages."

- "It's not my job to offer advice."

- "Couples have to work out their own solutions."

- "It depends what you mean by track record. Some relationships are best ended."

In this case, you should thank them for their time and try somebody else. Not only might they prove unhelpful, but what they have to say might even be potentially destructive. Paul and Jane did the right thing in leaving straight away.

The kind of answers you are looking for should be profoundly optimistic but with sensible qualifications:

- "Yes, of course. I will treat your marriage with the same importance that you do."

- "When I've heard your story, there may be some practical skills I can show you that other people have said they find helpful. I use them in my own marriage."

- "Of the couples who have more than one session with me, about two-thirds are still together and say they are happier six months later."

- "I'm afraid I don't follow couples up, but what I can say is that most leave here with a little more hope than when they came in."

Appendix: "I've tried telling him"

"I've tried telling him but it's no good. He just doesn't listen."

It's the universal cry of despair that receives an all-knowing look from other women.

"I know what it's like," women acknowledge one another. "I understand the years of frustration. If only he would be just that little bit more considerate or thoughtful. If only he would meet some of those unmet needs. If only he could occasionally fulfil some of those hopes and expectations that have long since fallen short."

"I really get the deep-seated anger and resentment that can stand it no longer," women tell one another. "I can relate to the numbness of despair, the loss of hope that anything will ever change. I even get that the relationship may have tipped over the edge beyond the point of caring, or believing, or wanting, that anything will ever change."

But are you sure you ever actually told him all this?

Sure, you may think you've made it obvious. You've hinted at it. He should have known. He should have seen. He should have noticed.

But he hasn't. And there's the teeniest possibility that he simply hasn't a clue. Even if men and women aren't always from Mars and Venus, being a different kind of human may make it hard for him to know what you want.

Here's Harry's own Mars and Venus statement:

Men don't do hints!

As a man, I certainly don't. If Kate wants me to do something, it's no good giving me a hint. What I need is a manual that tells me what to do and how to do it. Give me clear instructions, written in crayon, pinned to the fridge, and I can deliver.

***

It was sad, though no big shock, to hear from our friend Anna that she had walked out on her husband, Andrew. They had been married for twenty-five years.

Andrew was very much a man's man, a solid and reliable provider at work and a useful handyman at home, charming and entertaining to Anna and to his friends when he wanted to be, but often unpredictable and prickly, occasionally even sharp and dismissive. Despite his many good qualities, he was not a natural romantic and probably not the easiest man on earth to live with.

Nor was Anna a shrinking violet. For the most part, she came across as utterly lovely. Warm and welcoming to all, she had her fair share of idiosyncrasies. Anna noticed details, good and bad. But her observations tended to focus less on what was right and more on what was wrong, such as a picture hanging at a slight angle, a cushion that needed plumping, a vase facing the wrong way. It wasn't obsessive. But it seemed like a relentless pursuit of getting things right that came across as picky and negative.

Personally, either of them would have driven me mad. But Andrew and Anna had married each other, and not me.

Their marriage was more practical and utilitarian than emotional and romantic, an arrangement that most likely worked better for him than for her. There was definitely a real sense of love between them. There was a deep familiarity and comfort with one another. But it wasn't a soft and attractive love. Whereas he could escape from the things that irritated him by going to work or fixing things at home, she felt the lack of romantic love most acutely. They'd had a couple of marital blips along the way. Nothing too dramatic. As far as I knew, there had been no affairs.

It was a stray comment from Andrew – this is how I am, take it or leave it – that proved to be the last straw. For Anna, it was the death of hope that some day her husband might change. She packed her bags.

In the six months since leaving, their relationship had alternated between warm and fractious, much as if she had never left. With no obvious plan either for getting back together or for divorce, they were now stuck in limbo. Almost inevitably, both were still involved in each other's lives, though not in a healthy way. He expressed unhappiness with some of her new plans, as if he still had a right to comment on her personal life. She expressed concern for his well-being, as if she were still guardian of his health.

Many men fail to read the signs or take note of the hints that their wife is unhappy until it's too late. Worse, when a woman finally makes that mental decision to leave, she may become more at peace with herself and stop chasing him to change. He then notices the drop in pressure and thinks things are going well. When she eventually walks out, the shock knocks him for six. Finally realizing what he's lost, he will jump through hoops to win her back.

Andrew hadn't jumped at all. His reaction was worse: he did nothing. He didn't come running after her. He didn't burst into uncontrollable tears or get down on his knees and beg her not to leave. He quietly acquiesced. "If that's what you want," he told her.

When I first heard about this, I was amazed. He must have known what he was losing. I wondered if he already had one foot out of the door himself. But Anna was certain that he wasn't having an affair. Instead, his lack of response made her worry all the more that he was disappearing inside himself.

It seemed to me that they were now trapped in an unhappy separation, with no prospect of resolution. Both of them were now drifting purposelessly onwards without any hope or plan for either restoring their marriage or drawing it to a close.

I suggested to Anna that she needed to find a way out of this unsatisfactory state of limbo. She agreed. Alas, divorce seemed the only possible option. Bearing in mind Andrew's lack of response, making their marriage work in a new and better way seemed unimaginable to her.

"What if the reason he's not coming after you is that he simply doesn't know how?" I asked her. "Maybe he's a rabbit caught in the headlights."

"I've tried telling him what I need."

"Men don't do hints!" I replied. "It's going to be tough enough bringing years of marriage to an end without additional regrets that you didn't try everything. If only I'd done this; if only I'd done that. So give him a last chance. Write him a letter spelling it all out. This is what I need. This is what it looks like. This is what difference it will make."

We talked it through and came up with something like this.

***

Darling Andrew,

It's been six months since I walked out on you. There's going to come a time soon when we either need to draw our marriage to a close or find a way of making it work in a way that I can't even imagine right now. I want you to be free to live your own life – with or without me – just as I hope you will want me to be free to live mine – with or without you. But, right now, it feels like we're in limbo, neither fully together nor fully apart.

I am writing this because I want a resolution. At the moment we are sleepwalking towards a divorce. My worst fear is that we end up divorced and yet I will be forever plagued with regrets and "what ifs". "What if Andrew really wanted to find a way back but simply didn't know how?" "What if I'd only ever given hints when he wanted more practical ideas?" You may have lots of reasons why you don't ever want me back. You may even know perfectly well what you'd need to do. But I'm not confident of that.

This letter is written on the off chance that you are stuck like a rabbit in the headlights, frozen into inaction, desperately needing some clear instructions on how you might begin to win me back but not even knowing how, or daring to ask.

Even if I can't see even a faint possibility of making our marriage work, I wanted to make it crystal clear to you what I would need for that to happen. If you already know this, then it's all over and we need to end it as clearly and as painlessly as we can. I am deeply sad, but both of us can move on. If you don't, then the ball is in your court. You will have to fight hard to win me back. And you will have to keep fighting hard to keep me. I'm worth it. But I need to know beyond all doubt that you think I'm worth it.

So here's what might work, assuming you wanted to try, and with no guarantees that I will respond.

The first thing I need is your respect. I can't even quite believe I'm telling you this. Respect seems so central to any relationship, let alone the most intimate relationship of all. Respect says I have value. I have worth. I am somebody who matters. When I speak, I'm worth listening to. When I walk into the room, I'm worth stopping to look at.

You know how to show respect. There are several people in your life that you respect. Most obviously, your father. Maybe part of the reason is that, like you, he is a very decent man. But I suspect the real reason you respect him is simply that he is your father. You have looked up to him and admired him since you were a child.

I don't need you to look up to me. But I do need you to recognize me as a valuable human being in whom you are interested. That means you actively seek out my opinions, because they should matter to you. When I talk to you, I should feel that nobody else matters. That is what respect looks like.

I've had so much respect for you in the past. For so many years of our marriage, I've wanted to hear what you've had to say, no matter what the subject. It's faded at the moment because my respect wasn't reciprocated by you. I really don't care if it seems unfair that you are the one who will have to kick-start respect for me. All I can tell you is that if you begin to show me respect, my respect for you will return. This is not about fairness. This is about whether you want me back. You act. I'll respond.

The second thing I need is to be cherished. I love that word. To be cherished means to be cared for. Whatever is on my mind, however I'm feeling, matters.

Cherishing begins with asking how I slept last night. It continues with what you can do for me again and again. Being asked how you can make my day sunnier would be the nicest thing in the world to me. Cherishing means you care for my well-being. That means asking whether I still have that headache or whether I'm worried about the hospital appointment on Wednesday. Those little things show you have taken the trouble to find out what's on my mind, you notice, and you care. I'm top of your list of people that matter.

And, in case you think I am making a ball and chain for you, that couldn't be further from my mind. I would never abuse your generosity of spirit. Why would I? I think I would be overwhelmed even if I saw you making only the tiniest effort to care about me. I would only ever notice and appreciate the opportunities you take, never keeping score of the opportunities you miss. It's the things you do for me that count and not the things you don't. I don't expect constant mollycoddling; I just need to know you care about me.

The third thing is that I want you to fight for me and to keep fighting. It should be a total disaster that I've walked out on you. So tell me that your world has fallen apart. Tell me you would do anything to bring our marriage back to life. And you'd do it for me. Whatever it takes. I might not believe you there and then. After all, I walked out for a reason. But when you pursue me without begging, when you show me respect, when you show me you can cherish me, then maybe – just maybe – there's a chance.

And, fourthly, I want us to be a team. Of course we'll still have our own interests. That's fine. I'd just like us to do more things together. Like planning and cooking the food together when we have guests, rather than assuming I'll do it. Or like organizing the wine together, rather than me assuming you'll do it. Like being interested in each other's work, offering to help in any way, even if that only means carrying things to the car, and being delighted with the little things we can do together.

I started this letter being unable to imagine any kind of way ahead for us. Divorce seemed the only option. And yet, just writing about how it could be if you really wanted to put me first and make it work gives me the tiniest inkling that it's possible.

Have I been clear enough for you? I hope so. And I hope you think it's worth the risk of coming after me. We have too much history to consign it to the rubbish bin. I don't want to have to start again. But I do want something better. And if you can't or don't want to make it work in a way neither of us can imagine, then I will start again.

What I'm not telling you is to give up other things that are important to you. I don't want to make your life a misery. There's no penance to pay. But I do want to see you change your attitude to me. I want you to see me as number one in your life, the person who makes life worth living for you, the highlight of your every waking moment. If you can think like that about me, then the way you treat me will be no great burden. You'll want to do things differently, better, unimaginably so.

Loving me shouldn't be painful. It shouldn't be onerous. It should be fun. After all, that's how young couples woo one another. They give up other options to put each other first. If you can put me first, then maybe there is hope and I can forgive whatever is past and we can rebuild.

So now the ball is in your court. I've told you what I'd

*need. I don't actually think it's very much. I just want to
be treated as if I'm a bit special. I'm your wife, for heaven's
sake. I should stand out from the crowd a bit.*

*Ask your friends, ask my friends, if you need more help.
The friends I talk to understand and accept my decision
to leave. But all of them would rather there was a better
future for us together. So don't assume that they are on my
side and against you, just as I'm not against you. They're
not. They're on our side. Talk to them. They'll help you.*

*I want to be sure we haven't left any stones unturned.
Now it's up to you.*

With love,

Anna

***

Is there a postscript to this?

We don't know, because it hasn't happened yet.

Some couples can and do get back together after going
through a torrid time. Some don't. All we know is that,
whatever caused her to walk out in the first place, Anna has
now given Andrew a clear set of instructions for how to win
her back.

He may not respond, in which case they won't build the
new marriage that Anna can't even imagine right now. They
will end up divorced. Anna will undoubtedly regret that her
marriage failed. But at least she will be able to sleep free from
a further regret: "If only Andrew had known what to do, there
might have been a ray of hope."

Now she's told him what to do. Now the choice is his.

Notes

Chapter Four: For the sake of the children?

1. Data from the UK household survey Understanding Society, conducted during 2010–11, shows that 45% of teens aged thirteen to fifteen do not live with both natural parents; 42% live with one parent whereas 3% live with neither. Benson, H. (2013) *The myth of "long-term stable relationships" outside marriage*. Cambridge: Marriage Foundation.

2. The Relationships Foundation provides an annual estimate of how much money the UK taxpayer spends on picking up the pieces of family breakdown. The majority goes on benefits to lone-parent families above and beyond what one might expect for couple families. The latest figure came in at £48 billion, one-third higher than the 2016 UK defence budget of £34 billion. Ashcroft, J. (2016) *Counting the Cost of Family Failure, 2016 Update*. Cambridge: Relationships Foundation.

3. There's a great deal of evidence that married couples are more likely to stay together than cohabiting couples. While it's impossible to test whether marriage itself makes the difference, rather than the kind of people who marry, it is possible to compare parents while taking into account background factors. Just three out of ten parents who don't marry will still be together for their child's sixteenth birthday, compared with nearly eight out of ten parents who were already married. Once the baby was born, mother's age and education made no difference to this. Benson, H. (2015) *Get married BEFORE you have children*. Cambridge: Marriage Foundation.

4. This was really the first study to challenge the idea that

marital unhappiness is permanent. Nor did staying together typically trap unhappy couples in violent marriages: just 7% reported any kind of physical violence during the subsequent five years. So, in a study of 5,232 married adults, 645 were unhappy, some 500 of these remained together, and just thirty-five of these reported that their arguments got physical. It's awful for the couples involved, but it's a much smaller number than most might assume. Waite, L. et al. (2002) *Does Divorce Make People Happy? Findings from a Study of Unhappy Marriages.* New York: Institute for American Values.

5. A new analysis of data from the Millennium Cohort Study – not yet published at the time of writing – shows that new parents who are the unhappiest and consider themselves most on the brink are doing just as well ten years later as those who say they are happiest and least on the brink. The parents most likely to split up are the ones in the middle who are neither especially happy and secure nor especially unhappy and worried. Benson, H. & McKay, S. (in press) *Couples on the Brink.* Cambridge: Marriage Foundation.

6. Due to be published by Marriage Foundation alongside this book.

7. The government-run Families and Children Study is the definitive guide to differences in outcome between couple and lone-parent families. Prior to 2003, the annual analyses also covered differences between married and unmarried couple families. Alas we have to look elsewhere for this now. Maplethorpe, N. et al. (2010) *Families with Children in Britain: Findings from the 2008 Families and Children Study (FACS).* DWP RR 656.

8. Parenting styles are usually classed as authoritative (a balance of love and boundaries), authoritarian (less love and more boundaries), or permissive (more love and fewer boundaries). A UK study of 1,431 parents found that 53% of two-parent families were authoritative – which tends to have the best outcomes for children – compared to only 32% of lone-parent families. Lone parents were nearly twice as likely

to be permissive (28% vs 16%). Chan, T. W. & Koo, A. (2011) Parenting style and youth outcomes in the UK. *European Sociological Review* 27, 385–399.

9. Even those who take a more upbeat view acknowledge that children of divorce are more likely to experience serious negative outcomes. The debate is over whether the majority cope better with the negative effects or whether the negative effects are exaggerated. Hetherington, E. & Kelly, J. (2002) *For Better or Worse: Divorce Reconsidered*. New York: Norton.

10. Among 189 studies surveyed for this OECD review paper, 94% of the non-US studies and 88% of the US studies found negative effects of divorce on children. Chapple, S. & Richardson, D. (2009) *Doing Better for Children*. OECD.

11. Two detailed studies, of 944 and 270 divorced families respectively, have demolished the myth that co-operative co-parenting – the key ingredient in the so-called "good divorce" – can mitigate the effects of divorce on children. It doesn't. Amato, P., Kane, J. & James, S. (2011) Reconsidering the "Good Divorce". *Family Relations* 60, 511–524; and Beckmeyer, J., Coleman, M. & Ganong, L. (2014) Postdivorce Coparenting Typologies and Children's Adjustment. *Family Relations* 63, 526–537.

12. Most people's reaction is surprise when they are told that it's the "low-conflict" divorces that damage children most. This is invariably followed by a moment of revelation when they hear that it's because the children don't see it coming. This is the study that first established this remarkable finding, which every parent should know. Booth, A. & Amato, P. (2001) Parental pre-divorce relations and offspring post-divorce well-being. *Journal of Marriage & Family* 63, 197–212.

13. It's another big surprise to learn that the vast majority of couples who split up were not even remotely at each other's throats. On this basis, a great deal of family breakdown ought to be much more avoidable. The UK findings are similar to those in the US. Benson, H. & James, S. (2015) *Out of the Blue:*

Family Breakdown in the UK. Cambridge: Marriage Foundation; and James, S. (2015) Variation in marital quality in a national sample of divorced women. *Journal of Family Psychology*, 29, 479–489.

14. Here's what Professor Paul Amato has to say about the research on mediation: "The researchers found that mediation resulted in greater satisfaction with post-divorce outcomes, more contact between non-resident fathers and children, more communication between divorced parents, and less conflict between divorced parents. Despite these beneficial outcomes, most research on mediation continues to be plagued by methodological limitations, including the use of small samples and the absence of appropriate comparison groups. Moreover, existing research has not provided evidence that mediation actually benefits children." Amato, P. (2010) Research on divorce: Continuing trends and new developments. *Journal of Marriage and Family* 72, 650–666.

Chapter Five: Happy wife, happy life

1. Even if widely criticized in the academic world, it's still the "all-time best-selling hardcover non-fiction book", according to the publishers. Gray, J. (1992). *Men are from Mars, Women are from Venus*. New York, NY: Harper Collins.

2. This is one of the most comprehensive attempts to investigate behavioural differences between men and women. Spanning thirteen studies and 13,301 individuals, it acknowledges that there are differences on average. However, these mostly involve overlap rather than categorical differences, or "taxons", as the authors describe them. Carothers, B. & Reis, H. (2012) Men and women are from earth: Examining the latent structure of gender. *Journal of Personality and Social Psychology*. Online first publication, 22 October 2012; doi: 10.1037/a0030437.

3. The demand–withdraw pattern of communication, where

one partner is critical and demanding while the other is withdrawn and avoidant, has been linked to lower marital quality and divorce since the 1990s. This study shows that the phenomenon holds true in the different cultures of Brazil, Italy, Taiwan, and the US. Christensen, A. et al. (2006) Cross-cultural consistency of the demand/withdraw interaction pattern in couples. *Journal of Marriage and Family* 68, 1029–1044.

4. Benson, H. (2013) *Let's Stick Together: The Relationship Book for New Parents* (2nd edition). Oxford: Lion Hudson.

5. Benson, H. (2009) Back off or fire back? Negative relationship behaviours amongst postnatal married and cohabiting couples. In H. Benson and S. Callan (eds) *What Works in Relationship Education: Lessons from Academics and Service Deliverers in the United States and Europe* (pp. 55–66). Doha, Qatar: Doha International Institute for Family Studies and Development.

6. Carothers and Reis (2012).

7. *Let's Stick Together* is a one-hour relationship programme for ante-natal and post-natal groups, written and developed by Harry. It is now run across the UK by the charity Care for the Family: www.careforthefamily.org.uk/courses-lets-stick-together.

8. This Oxford study followed fifteen fathers from two months before to six months after their baby was born. It suggests that fathers are "prevented" from fulfilling their desire to be involved by a combination of societal attitudes, economic and healthcare barriers, and government policies. Machin, A. (2015) Mind the gap: The expectation and reality of involved fatherhood. *Fathering* 13, 36–59.

9. My Family Care (2016) Shared parental leave: Where are we now? See: https://www.myfamilycare.co.uk/news/update/shared-parental-leave-where-are-we-now.html

10. Since 1997, the proportion of mothers who would prefer

not to work at all has fallen from 26% to 20%. However, those who wish to work part-time has increased very slightly from 30% to 32%. Wang, W. (2013) Mothers and work: What's ideal? Washington: Pew Research Center. See: http://www.pewresearch.org/fact-tank/2013/08/19/mothers-and-work-whats-ideal/

11. One might assume that mothers would be happiest with their life if they worked part-time because that allows the best balance of home and work life. One might also assume that part-time work would be least satisfying, perhaps because the pay and prospects are lower than with full-time work. In fact, the reverse is the case. Mothers are happiest with life if they work full-time but happiest with their job if they work part-time. It's a puzzle! Booth, A. & van Ours, J. (2008) Job satisfaction and family happiness: The part-time work puzzle. *The Economic Journal* 118, 77–99.

12. In a US survey of 1,040 working parents, 40% of women said being a working parent made it harder to get on in the workplace while 45% said it made it harder to be a good parent. In contrast, just 15% of working fathers said it was harder to get on at work (12% said it made it easier), while 31% said it made it harder to be a good parent (15% said it was easier). Taylor, P. et al. (2013) On Pay Gap, Millennial Women Near Parity – For Now. Washington: Pew Research Center. See: http://www.pewsocialtrends.org/2013/12/11/on-pay-gap-millennial-women-near-parity-for-now/

13. A survey by Direct Line Insurance, reported in the *Daily Mail*, 10 April 2014, found that seven out of ten mothers reckon they never get a day off to unwind and spend time with their family. Four out of five spend more time on chores than with their children. The good news is that men are doing more of their fair share, according to another survey by Karcher, reported in the *Daily Mail*, 22 March 2015. Half of all men reckon they do more than their father did, whereas 41% of women reckon they do less than their mum.

14. This data was specially commissioned by us for this book

but is publicly available through the ONS website. Among families with the youngest children, newborns to under four, the proportion of one-earner families was 37% in 1999, falling slightly to 33% in 2014, fifteen years later. Among families with older children, aged four to ten, the proportion of one-earner families rose slightly from 24% to 26%. The proportion also rose slightly from 20% to 21% for families with teen children, aged eleven to eighteen. Among families with the youngest children, the proportion has fallen slightly from 94% to 90%. Among families with older children, the proportion rose slightly from 86% to 87%. And among those with teens, the proportion also rose from 75% to 79%. Office for National Statistics (2015) Families with dependent children by number of children, UK, 1996 to 2014.

15. In a study of 722 older husbands and wives, husbands reported that they were happier with both marriage and life when their wives were also happy with their marriage. Happy husbands didn't seem to have the same effect on their wives. Carr, D., Freedman, V., Cornman, J. & Schwarz, N. (2014) Happy marriage, happy life? Marital quality and subjective well-being in later life. *Journal of Marriage and Family* 76: 930–948.

16. A study of 385 mothers and their children showed that when mums were happy in their marriage, their children tended to be more positive in their emotional expressiveness and less negative. Froyen, L., Skibbe, L., Bowles, R., Blow, A. & Gerde, H. (2013) Marital satisfaction, family emotional expressiveness, home learning environments, and children's emergent literacy. *Journal of Marriage and Family* 75, 42–55.

17. A study of 1,998 married men and women showed that those who stayed happier over time were also happier with life in general and showed fewer signs of depression. Kamp Dush, C., Taylor, M. & Kroeger, R. (2008) Marital happiness and psychological well-being across the life course. *Family Relations* 57, 211–226.

18. In a study of 453 teenagers who were living with their

mother but not their father, both parents had an influence on their behaviour and well-being. Whereas the father's influence was modest, the mother's influence tended to be the stronger. King, V. & Sobolewski, J. (2006) Nonresident fathers' contributions to adolescent well-being. *Journal of Marriage and Family* 68, 537–557.

19. In a study of 685 Dutch couples, the only transmission of values within couples over a five-year period was from wives to husbands. This only happened among couples who were happy in their marriage. Roest, A., Semon Dubas, J., Gerris, J. & Engels, R. (2006) Disentangling value similarities and transmissions in established marriages: A cross-lagged longitudinal study. *Journal of Marriage and Family* 68, 1132–1146.

20. In a study of 126 couples throughout their first six years of marriage, changes in the way they felt about their marriage during this time tended to point to how happy they were with their life at the end of six years. This also applies to both husbands and wives. Stanley, S., Ragan, E., Rhoades, G. & Markman, H. (2012) Examining changes in relationship adjustment and life satisfaction in marriage. *Journal of Family Psychology* 26, 165–170.

Chapter Six: What mums want

1. The concept of couple identity goes back to the biblical concept of covenant, wherein two people exchange their old identity for a new one. Modern research finds that those with a strong sense of identity as a couple – who use words like "we/ours" rather than "I/you/mine/yours" – tend to be more personally committed. Stanley, S. & Markman, H. (1992) Assessing commitment in personal relationships. *Journal of Marriage and Family* 54, 595–608.

2. Professor Scott Stanley and colleagues at the University of Denver have developed the dedication/constraints model of commitment. This paper gives a fuller description and – at

time of writing – is available free online. Stanley, S., Rhoades, G. & Whitton, S. (2010) Commitment: Functions, formation, and the securing of romantic attachment. *Journal of Family Theory & Review* 2, 243–257.

3. Calculating divorce rates is a remarkably complex subject. We want to know what will happen in the future to couples who are married today, yet the only data we have is on what has happened to them in the past. So what we have to do is look at couples by year of marriage, see how many have divorced so far, then add on the latest rates for couples who have been married longer. UK data is very good for working this out. The Office for National Statistics estimates today's risk at 42%. But if we include overseas weddings – which adds another 10–15% weddings in each year – the real rate is nearer 38%. US national data is not as good and so estimates have to come from surveys. One reputable study estimates this at around 42–45%; however, the whole subject remains fraught with debate about how to do the sums. Benson, H. (2016) *Vanishing Divorce*. Cambridge: Marriage Foundation; and Schoen, R. & Canudas-Romo, V. (2006) Timing effects on divorce: 20th century experience in the United States. *Journal of Marriage and Family* 68(3), 749–758.

4. Understanding Society is an annual survey of 40,000 UK households, within which 1,783 mothers had children aged fourteen or fifteen. Of those mothers who had been married before their child was born, 76% were still together with the child's father. Of those who got married after their child's birth, 44% were still together. Of those who had never married, 31% were still together. After Harry published these findings in a report for Marriage Foundation, the social affairs editor of a major national paper wrote back to him in an email, "It is a great piece of research and this sort of data will change behaviour. What couple can now argue it doesn't matter if they are married or not when they start a family?" Benson, H. (2015) *Get married BEFORE you have children*. Cambridge: Marriage Foundation.

5. Marriages seem to be happier if a lot of people have been to the wedding. This is not an effect of money, but purely of the number of people. Why does this happen? It could be either that people with stronger social networks have happier marriages, or the other way round: that having more people at the wedding affirms the couple in the choice they have made and that these people then provide social support afterwards. Francis, A. & Mialon, H. (2015) "A diamond is forever" and other fairy tales: The relationship between wedding expenses and marriage duration. *Economic Inquiry* 53, 1919–1930; and Rhoades, G. & Stanley, S. (2014) *Before "I Do": What Do Premarital Experiences Have to Do with Marital Quality Among Today's Young Adults?* Virginia: National Marriage Project.

6. It's an astonishing finding. Pretty well all of the change in UK divorce rates since the 1960s has taken place during the early years of marriage and among divorces granted to wives. In other words, there has been no change at all in divorces granted to husbands over any duration of marriage, nor any change in divorce rates once couples pass their first decade. Policy-makers who want to see less divorce should recognize that the only aspect of marriage stability that seems changeable is how men behave in those first few years. Benson, H. (2015) *Happy Families: Men Behaving Better*. Cambridge: Marriage Foundation.

7. It's well worth tracking down an online copy of this masterpiece from the world's top relationship research team at the University of Denver. Using the everyday language of "sliding", "deciding", and "inertia" – getting stuck – suddenly makes it very easy to understand the two sides of commitment. Stanley, S., Rhoades, G. & Markman, H. (2006) Sliding versus deciding: Inertia and the premarital cohabitation effect. *Family Relations* 55: 499–509.

8. All being well, the full findings of this survey should have come out by the time as this book is launched, via www.marriagefoundation.org.uk

9. Before having children, women seem to be generally happy

when their husband works long hours and enjoys his job – because he is investing in their future. After having children, however, this same hard-working husband is now perceived as abandoning his wife at home with the children. The husband hasn't changed. But, to the mother, the present reality of looking after children on her own seems to trump the distant prospect of more money in the bank. Van Steenbergen, E., Kluwer, E. & Karney, B. (2011) Workload and the trajectory of marital satisfaction in newlyweds: Job satisfaction, gender, and parental status as moderators. *Journal of Family Psychology* 25, 345–355.

Chapter Seven: Learning to love

1. The first claim to be able to predict how couples will do simply by watching them discuss a difficult issue for just a few minutes was made in 1992. There are good reasons for imagining that the seeds of success are present early on in a relationship, but there are equally good reasons – not least that life happens – for being sceptical that this can be predicted with such accuracy. This 1998 study by John Gottman and colleagues received a barrage of criticism in the same journal in which it was published. Gottman, J., Coan, J., Carrere, S. & Swanson, C. (1998). Predicting marital happiness and stability from newlywed interactions. *Journal of Marriage and the Family* 60, 5–22.

2. It turns out the mathematical formula that accurately predicts the outcomes of one particular group of couples doesn't work nearly as well with another group. This study demonstrated they could predict how well one group did over thirteen years of marriage with 77% accuracy – which is still not bad – but this dropped to 62% when they applied the same formula to a different group of couples. This might still sound good but in fact it isn't useful at all. All of us can predict with 58% accuracy simply by saying every couple will be happy! Clements, M., Stanley, S. & Markman, H. (2004) Before they

said "I do": Discriminating amongst marital outcomes over 13 years. *Journal of Marriage & Family* 66, 613–626.

3. Gottman, J. & Levenson, R. (2000) The timing of divorce: Predicting when a couple will divorce over a 14-year period. *Journal of Marriage and Family* 62, 737–745.

4. These are just some of the factors highlighted by Scott Stanley that are known to increase the risk of distress or divorce: neuroticism, premarital cohabitation, parental divorce, communication withdrawal and invalidation, escalation and defensiveness, higher ratios of hostility to warmth, difficulties in communication and problem solving, knowing partner a short time before marriage, separate finances, marrying young, lower education, and remarriage. Stanley, S. (2001) Making a case for premarital education. *Family Relations* 50, 272–280.

5. The best studies and reviews of marriage preparation research have found no evidence of differences between those who attend courses and those who don't. Even if there was, with divorce rates at 40–50%, it's arguable that pretty well every couple is at risk to some extent. Carroll, J. & Doherty, W. (2003) Evaluating the effectiveness of premarital prevention programs: A meta-analytic review of outcome research. *Family Relations* 52, 105–118; and Stanley, S., Amato, P., Johnson, C. & Markman, H. (2006) Premarital education, marital quality, and marital stability: Findings from a large, random household survey. *Journal of Family Psychology* 20, 117–126.

6. There are plenty of review papers that summarize the evidence that relationship programmes improve relationship quality, reduce conflict, and reduce divorce over up to five years. See Carroll & Doherty (2003) and Markman, H. & Rhoades, G. (2012) Relationship education research: Current status and future directions. *Journal of Marital and Family Therapy* 38, 169–200; and Hawkins, A. & Erickson, S. (2015) Is couple and relationship education effective for lower income participants? A meta-analytic study. *Journal of Family Psychology* 29, 59–68.

7. The Stanley, Amato, Johnson & Markman (2006) study was based on a random telephone survey of 2,000 married couples, of whom one-third had completed a marriage preparation course of some kind. The findings – that divorce rates were roughly 31% lower among the couples who did a course – held up regardless of race, income, and education. The conclusion is that marriage preparation is generally beneficial for a wide range of couples.

8. Arguably the most comprehensive gold-standard study of relationship education ever took place on two US military bases in the late 2000s: 662 couples were randomly assigned either to a three-day course, Strong Bonds, or to a control group. On one of the bases the course appeared to have no effect at all. But on the larger base – where the average age and income of participants was lower and service personnel were more likely to be about to deploy to Iraq – divorce rates over the subsequent two years were 8%, versus 15% for the non-course group. Stanley, S. et al. (2014) A randomized controlled trial of relationship education in the US Army: 2-year outcomes. *Family Relations* 63, 482–495.

9. For more on *Let's Stick Together,* see www.careforthefamily. org.uk/courses-lets-stick-together

10. When we ran relationship courses, we would always start by asking couples what they thought was most important. The word "communication" usually came up first or second. Learning how to communicate better is also the single thing that couples say they found most useful. For example, three-quarters of men and women attending the PREP relationship course picked "speaker–listener" as the top thing they learned. Stanley, S. et al. (2001) Community-based premarital prevention: Clergy and lay leaders on the front lines. *Family Relations* 50, 67–76.

11. See www.5lovelanguages.com by Gary Chapman.

12. Benson, H. (2013) *Let's Stick Together: The Relationship Book for New Parents* (2nd edition). Oxford: Lion Hudson.

13. Benson, H. (2013), ibid.

14. Benson, H. & McKay, S. (in press) *Date Nights*. Cambridge: Marriage Foundation.

15 Claxton, A. & Perry-Jenkins, M. (2008) No fun anymore: Leisure and marital quality across the transition to parenthood. *Journal of Marriage and Family* 70, 28–43.

16. Hook, J. (2012) Working on the weekend: Fathers' time with family in the United Kingdom. *Journal of Marriage and Family* 74, 631–642.

17. Dew, J. & Wilcox, W. (2011) If momma ain't happy: Explaining declines in marital satisfaction among new mothers. *Journal of Marriage and Family* 73, 1–12.

Chapter Eight: For better, for worse

1. Wilcox, W. & Dew, J. (2010). Is love a flimsy foundation? Soulmate versus institutional models of marriage. *Social Science Research* 39, 687–699.

2. The much-cited US study found that viewing their marriage as "sacred" or "God-inspired" was associated with more collaboration, less conflict and verbal aggression, and less stalemate during arguments. Mahoney, A., et al. (1999) Marriage and the spiritual realm: The role of proximal and distal religious constructs in marital functioning. *Journal of Family Psychology* 13, 321–338. Another new UK study by Harry and Professor Steve McKay for Marriage Foundation – not yet published at the time of writing – backs up this point that it's not religion that matters but how you "do" marriage. Over the first eleven years of parenthood, the chance of staying together appears to favour religious couples. But, once marriage is taken into account, religion has no effect at all. In other words, religious couples tend to be more stable only because they are more likely to get married.

Chapter Nine: I love you and want to be close to you

1. Studies of attribution have been around for a long time, pioneered by Professor Frank Fincham, currently at Florida State University. These show a strong link between the way couples attribute behaviour and how satisfied they are in their marriage. In this study, he demonstrated that attribution influences marriage, and not vice versa. Fincham, F., Harold, G. & Gano-Phillips, S. (2000) The longitudinal association between attributions and marital satisfaction: Direction of effects and role of efficacy expectations. *Journal of Family Psychology* 14, 267–285. More recent enquires have shown that attributions are most likely borne out of attachment insecurity. Kimmes, J. et al. (2015) The role of pessimistic attributions in the association between anxious attachment and relationship satisfaction. *Family Relations* 64, 547–562.

2. Papp, L., Cummings, E. & Goeke-Morey, M. (2009) For richer, for poorer: Money as a topic of marital conflict in the home. *Family Relations* 58, 91–103.

3. The bad habit of reacting negatively during conflict tends to predict divorce in the early years, but not the later years. In contrast, the good habit of reacting positively during both conflict and everyday discussions tends to predict divorce in the later years, but not the early years. Gottman, J. & Levenson, R. (2000) The timing of divorce: Predicting when a couple will divorce over a 14-year period. *Journal of Marriage and Family* 62, 737–745.

4. Gottman, J. (1994) *What Predicts Divorce?* Hillsdale, NJ: Erlbaum.

5. There's a lot more information on the four danger signs – Escalation, Negative Interpretation, Invalidation, and Withdrawal – in this highly recommended book that first came out in 2001. Markman, H., Stanley, S. & Blumberg, S. (2010) *Fighting for Your Marriage: A Deluxe Revised Edition of the Classic Best-seller for Enhancing Marriage and Preventing Divorce.* John Wiley & Sons.

6. Christensen, A. et al. (2006) Cross-cultural consistency of the demand/withdraw interaction pattern in couples. *Journal of Marriage and Family* 68, 1029–1044.

7. Benson, H. (2009) Back off or fire back? Negative relationship behaviours amongst postnatal married and cohabiting couples. In H. Benson and S. Callan (eds) *What Works in Relationship Education: Lessons from Academics and Service Deliverers in the United States and Europe* (pp. 55–66). Doha, Qatar: Doha International Institute for Family Studies and Development.

8. Benson, H. (2013) *Let's Stick Together: The Relationship Book for New Parents* (2nd edition). Oxford: Lion Hudson.

9. This is the extraordinary counter-intuitive finding that every parent considering splitting up should know about. Children are often better off out of a high-conflict relationship. What they don't get is when a low-conflict one ends. It makes no sense. Children tend to do worst after the break-up of a low-conflict relationship. Booth, A. & Amato, P. (2001) Parental pre-divorce relations and offspring post-divorce well-being. *Journal of Marriage & Family* 63, 197–212. Read our shocking story of Judith in chapter four to see how this can go on to sabotage relationships once children become adults.

Chapter Ten: Back from the brink

1. Due to be published by Marriage Foundation alongside this book.

Chapter Eleven: Wise friends

1. Benson, H. & James, S. (2015) *Out of the Blue: Family Breakdown in the UK*. Cambridge: Marriage Foundation.

2. Although it leans perhaps a little too favourably towards counselling and less so towards relationship education, this

UK review by Tavistock Centre for Couple Relationships is excellent. Abse, S., Hewison, D., Casey, P. & Meier, R. (2015) *What Works in Relationship Support: An Evidence Review*. London: Tavistock.

3. Having established themselves as the most popular church-based courses in the UK, The Marriage Course and The Marriage Preparation Course are increasingly available around the world. See www.themarriagecourses.org

4. The best research studies into relationship education almost all involve PREP and its variants, which include Within My Reach for single mums and Strong Bonds for military couples. See www.prepinc.com

5. Marriage Encounter was arguably the pioneer of weekend marriage courses and has been around since the 1970s in various guises. Originally Catholic in orientation, there are versions in all sorts of denominations. Our big breakthrough happened on a United Marriage Encounter weekend in Taiwan! See www.wwme.org.uk and www.marriageencounter.org.uk

6. PREPARE and ENRICH are two inventories of statements to which couples respond yes, no, or don't know. The statements cover a huge range of topics. On completion, their responses form the basis for one or more discussion sessions with a facilitator/mentor couple. See www.prepare-enrich.co.uk

7. FOCCUS is another inventory of statements, very similar to PREPARE/ENRICH. In the UK, it's now used by the Catholic marriage preparation group Marriage Care. See www.marriagecare.org.uk

8. This study suggests that on average 60–75% see significant benefits, of whom half end up distressed or splitting up – leaving a net gain of some 30–40%. Johnson, S. & Lebow, J. (2000) The "coming of age" of couple therapy: A decade review. *Journal of Marital and Family Therapy* 26, 23–38.

9. Benson, H. (2015) *Get married BEFORE you have children*. Cambridge: Marriage Foundation.

10. This is a Swedish study claiming to find a positive effect from couple therapy. However, the authors not only acknowledge that different therapy approaches seem to produce the same outcomes; they also state that it would be unethical to use a "wait-list" comparison group because these couples wouldn't make progress. This rather dismisses the possibility that time can heal, which could be part of the reason some couples appear to benefit from couple therapy anyway. Lundblad, A. & Hansson, K. (2006) Couples therapy: Effectiveness of treatment and long-term follow-up. *Journal of Family Therapy* 28, 136–152.

11. Gottman, J. (1998) Psychology and the study of marital processes. *Annual Review of Psychology* 49, 169–197.

12. These questions are a short version of those advocated by US researcher and marital therapist Bill Doherty. He has long been trying to improve the quality of marital therapy. His talk at the 1999 Smartmarriages conference in Washington, DC is well worth a read. Doherty, W. (1999) How marital therapy can be hazardous to your health. See www.smartmarriages. com

LET'S STICK TOGETHER

The relationship book for new parents

"A great book written with warmth and a sense of humour. Full of good down-to-earth advice, it's a must for all couples, whatever age or background."

Rachel Waddilove, author of
The Baby Book, The Toddler Book* and *Sleep Solutions

Are you a new parent or about to become one?

Learn three simple habits that will keep love alive and protect your relationship against the pressures that parenting brings.

In the excitement and exhaustion of becoming parents, the first thing that can get overlooked is your relationship. You might spend less time together, argue over little things, drift apart...

So many families break up once the baby arrives. But it doesn't have to be like this. Most family breakdown is avoidable.

In *Let's Stick Together*, relationship educator and father of six Harry Benson guides you through three simple habits that research shows make or break new mums and dads. Illustrated with real-life examples from Harry's own back-from-the-brink marriage and those of other couples, *Let's Stick Together* highlights simple principles that will make your relationship the best it can be.

ISBN: 978-0-7459-5608-4 I e-ISBN: 978-0-7459-5780-7